FOOD

PETS

DIE

FOR

FOOD PETS DIE FOR

SHOCKING FACTS ABOUT PET FOOD

BY ANN N. MARTIN

FOREWORD BY DR. MICHAEL W. FOX

NEWSAGE PRESS, OREGON

Food Pets Die For:
Shocking Facts About Pet Food

Copyright © 1997 Ann N. Martin
ISBN 0-939165-31-7

Address Inquiries to:
NewSage Press
PO Box 607
Troutdale, OR 97060-0607
503-695-2211; fax: 503-695-5406
Email: newsage@teleport.com
Web Site: http://www.teleport.com/~newsage

Book design by John Rodal
Production Assistance by Nancy L. Doerrfeld-Smith

Printed in the United States on recycled paper with soy ink.
Distributed in the United States and Canada by Publishers Group West
1-800-788-2123

Library of Congress Cataloging-in-Publication Data

Martin, Ann N., 1944-
    Food pets die for : shocking facts about pet food / Ann N. Martin.
        p.   cm.
    Includes bibliographical references (   ) and index.
    ISBN   0-939165-31-7
    1. Pets---Feeding and feeds.   2. Pets--Health.   3.Pets--Feeding
and feeds--Contamination--United States.   4. Pets--Feeding and
feeds--Contamination--Canada.   5. Pet food industry--United States.
6. Pet food industry--Canada.
I. title.
SF414.M37   1997
363. 19'29--dc21
                                                        97-34729
                                                        CIP

2 3 4 5 6 7 8 9 10

DEDICATION

For my Dad, Emmett Nolan, who left a legacy of humor, patience, tenacity, and the fortitude to continue in the face of adversity.

Acknowledgments

A mere thank you seems so inadequate in expressing my gratitude to all the people who were instrumental in seeing this book reach fruition.

Dr. Michael Fox, Vice President, Bioethics and Farm Animal Protection, The Humane Society of the United States, my friend, my mentor. You have known and seen the injustices inflicted not only on our pets, but on all animals, and you have fought to right the wrongs. From your extremely busy schedule, from your own writing, you spent untold hours to help me. *Muchas gracias*.

Maureen R. Michelson, publisher of NewSage Press and Tracy Smith, senior editor, your patience, understanding, and professionalism have been admirable. Through our daily communication Tracy, you guided me, chapter by chapter, word by word, with the intent of making this book more readable. It was a true pleasure.

Dr. Richard Fox, you must know how very much your knowledge was appreciated during my research. You filled in the blanks, explained veterinary terminology, and suggested sources of information. For this and for the many years you cared for my pets, I'll be forever grateful.

Dr. Don Franco, you freely answered any questions I had on the rendering industry. Although there may not have been a meeting of minds on this issue, you were always honest and never condescending.

Jamie, my son, the last chapter has been written. You corrected my spelling but gave up on the grammatical errors. You taught me computer basics. You grew accustomed to frozen dinner when I did not have time to cook. Your help has been very much appreciated.

Joan and Linda, my friends, my sounding boards, my legal advisors. If I was stuck, you two always had the answers. Your interest in my research never wavered. Just think Joan, if we had won the court case this book would have never been written.

Mary, my sister, who listened every day to what had transpired in my search for information. Be assured that my entire life did not revolve around the pet food industry—it just seemed that way.

Drs. Wendell Belfield, Richard Pitcairn, and Tom Lonsdale, and, Catherine O'Driscoll, and John Watt, you gave of your time and kept me updated. The information continues to accumulate. With this book and all our efforts perhaps more pets will live longer, healthier, lives. To Torsten, my friend, thank you for being there.

And last but not least, Charlie my Newfoundland, and Simon, Jake, Ben, and Yakkie, my felines, my taste testers—you survived and are no doubt healthier for it.

Contents

Foreword

Ann Martin is to the pet food industry what Rachel Carson was to
the petrochemical-pesticide industry. In the same spirit of rigorous
investigation, Martin has revealed what ingredients go into pet food
and into the feed of most farm animals whose meat and other produce
we consume. *Food Pets Die For* is not an overstatement. It is more fac-
tually correct than the ingredient labels on cat and dog food, which
claim to be scientifically formulated and balanced for a pet's health
and maintenance. I trust Martin's science, and her methodology is
tenacious and direct. Martin's investigation into the pet food industry
(whose practices in North America are virtually identical throughout
Europe and the industrial world) asks crucial questions that must be
answered.

This is a very important book for a number of reasons. As a veterinarian and animal rights' advocate, I have long maintained that one of
the cornerstones of our companion animals' health is good nutrition.
This right and the health and welfare of our pets have been violated,
and will continue to be violated until responsible pet owners protest
loudly enough and hold the United States and Canadian governments
and the multinational pet food industry accountable for the contents of
commercial pet food. And pet owners must decide after reading this
book what they can do for their companion animals' diets, as well as
holding the pet food industry accountable to consumers.

Our pets and our families will benefit from food that comes from
good soil since organic farming rather than conventional agriculture
aims at keeping all the essential trace minerals and other essential
plant nutrients in the soil to produce healthy, nutritious crops. Martin
shows that making your own pets' diet from scratch with known ingredients, preferably without chemical additives like Ethoxyquin, BHT,
and propylene glycol, or animal waste by-products from rendering
plants, will do wonders for your pet's health.

Many readers will be in disbelief when they finish this book, but I
must reiterate, Martin has unveiled just one aspect of the agribusiness

food industry that affects our pets, our hearts, and our pockets. Agribusiness is an industry whose practices have not been subject to public accountability. But the time is now ripe for a revolution in agriculture as we, the public, take more control over how the food we purchase for our families, including our pets, has been produced and processed.

Begin today: **Read the label**—and don't buy any pet food that contains "meat meal," meat and poultry by-products, bone meal, animal fat, or tallow.

Dr. Michael W. Fox
Vice President of Bioethics and Farm
Animal Protection International
The Humane Society of the United States

Introduction

Until about seven years ago, I fed commercial pet food to my menagerie of cats, dogs, and rabbits. I did so because this is what my veterinarians recommended. This was, and still is, what the pet food industry assures us is a "complete and balanced diet" for our pets. Not one to question authority, I followed this advice until my two large dogs became ill after ingesting a commercial pet food. It was then that I began to ask questions. I am not a veterinarian. I am not an expert. But I am a concerned consumer, an individual who wanted answers to my questions. At the time, little did I know this personal investigation would lead to seven years of searching, and now, this book. Those first questions were basic:

Who regulates the pet food industry? What are the ingredients used in these foods? What tests are conducted to ascertain if these foods are complete and balanced? Can these foods have a detrimental effect on the health of our companion animals? What research is available showing that our pets cannot be fed human food and who has undertaken such research?

I have since learned that this industry is virtually self-regulated. Just about anything and everything is fair game for use in pet food. This includes condemned and contaminated material from slaughterhouse facilities, roadkill, dead, diseased, disabled, and dying animals picked up by dead-stock removal operations; and, although the industry vehemently denies it, euthanized companion animals. These are just the protein sources. Grains and fats, dregs from the human food chain, are also included.

When I convey the information I have unearthed to other pet owners or to the public at seminars, people are concerned, and shocked. Most people have no clue as to what they are feeding their pets. Most pet owners believe—as I once did—the information fostered by the pet food industry. I am here to offer the conclusion of my personal investigation. In my opinion, most pet food is garbage—unregulated garbage.

Whenever I speak publicly on this issue, I am swamped with questions. People want more information. Every day I receive phone calls, faxes, and email from all over the world. I have learned that little information is available on this industry. If it had not been for the illness of my dogs, I, too, would have been none the wiser.

I have written a number of articles for magazines in both the United States and Canada, but these articles barely scratch the surface of what is actually happening within the North American pet food industry. A book is the only viable means of putting my seven years (and still continuing) research together. As I was writing the book, more information was coming to light on a daily basis, especially the development on mad cow disease and its connection with commercial pet food. This has been added, but I am sure more revealing information will be forthcoming after we go to press.

Pets can do extremely well on homemade food, and it is my hope that in writing this book pet owners will take the time to cook for their dog or cat. When you open a can or bag of commercial pet food, question the quality of the ingredients. In this book I explain how to read labels on commercial pet food to understand what certain ingredients are. And if you do not have time to cook for your pets, at least you will know what to watch for—and avoid—when reading pet food labels. If you must buy commercial pet food, some are definitely better than others.

I hope that this book provides insight into an industry that is literally feeding millions of dogs and cats per year. If after reading this book, you cannot be dissuaded from feeding your pet commercial food, at least provide your pet with some fresh, raw food regularly. (Meat should always be cooked.) Could you or your children stay healthy on substandard food from a can or bag every day for the rest of your lives? Don't expect your pet to.

Chapter One

The Case Against Commercial Pet Food

Monday, January 22, 1990, was the beginning of an enlightening, frustrating, and shocking foray into the depths of the commercial pet food industry. At that point in time, my home was occupied by Louie, the Saint Bernard and Charlie, the Newfoundland, both five years old. The felines included three sealpoint Siamese, Yakkie, Ben, and Arthur; and one long-haired tabby, Felix. These guys were not just pets, they were an integral part of the family. Louie and Charlie had big cozy beds in the living room and the cats had their own beds complete with heating pads placed under big furry coverlets. All ate three meals a day: breakfast, lunch, and dinner.

On the fateful evening of January 22, I opened a new bag of dry, commercial pet food. This food was purchased, in bulk, two days previously. Neither Louie nor Charlie was a big eater, and I wanted to be sure that the food I was feeding them was relatively fresh. When I did my weekly shopping, I'd stop at the local feed store and pick up twelve or fifteen pounds of dry dog food.

On that evening, as was the regular routine, I put the food in the bowls, added hot water, let it cool, and gave it to the dogs. Both ate, went out for ten minutes, came back in, and went to sleep. After feeding the cats I went to watch television. Suddenly Louie jumped up and regurgitated most of the food he had eaten. I reasoned that he had just eaten too quickly and perhaps a little fresh air would make him feel better. Out we went into the cold snowy night. A walk around two or three blocks and I was ready to head home. Louie seemed to be feeling better, and it was nice to get back to a warm house.

As I was taking my boots off, I could hear Louie gulping down water from his bowl. Realizing that drinking all that water might not be the best thing for him, I called him back. Charlie proceeded to finish off the water. What was making them so thirsty? On the way to the kitchen I was startled to see that Charlie had also been ill while Louie and I had been out. The vomiting and heavy consumption of water continued through the night. The next day I talked with my veterinarian. His suggestion was to put them on a bland diet for a few days. He recommended a diet of ground beef or chicken, brown rice, and perhaps some grated carrots. After two days I became rather complacent; they were fine, and I went back to feeding them the commercial pet food.

Within one and a half hours the vomiting and excess water consumption began again. What was happening? No diarrhea, no other symptoms, just vomiting and drinking. Back to the bland diet and again, like a miracle, both dogs recovered. Two days on the bland diet, and I decided to do an experiment. This time I fed the commercial food to only Louie and left Charlie on the bland diet. I waited and if things followed true to form, Louie would become ill. Like clockwork, Louie began to vomit within one and a half hours. I concluded that it must be the food. This time Louie seemed worse than on previous occasions and I felt he needed veterinary attention.

Louie was not the most cooperative dog, and it took three of us to hold him for the veterinarian to draw blood. A physical exam showed nothing unusual, and Louie was given something to settle his stomach and sent home. That evening, the veterinarian evaluated the blood work and found nothing unusual. Charlie had remained fine through all of this, which gave the veterinarian and I a good indication that the dog food was suspect. From that day forward, neither dog was fed commercial pet food.

The veterinary bill was $110 (Canadian). I felt that the pet food manufacturer was responsible for this bill, and I fully expected the manufacturer to reimburse me. After sending the company the bill, a corporate representative replied, "Send us the remainder of the food and we'll have it tested."[1] I forwarded half of what remained to the company. The corporate representative was not pleased because he had requested the entire amount of the remaining food. However, a month later, I received the results of the test. Supposedly, because I had not provided enough of a sample, the company could only conduct a feed test, no analytical testing. Over a three-day span, it fed a ten-year old Siberian Husky approximately two pounds of dog food and nothing else. It stated that the dog ate normally with no signs of vomiting or diarrhea. I had never indicated that Louie or Charlie had developed diarrhea.

My veterinarian suggested that with the symptoms the dogs displayed, it could have been a mycotoxin (toxins produced by fungi when foods are stored in humidity), aflatoxin B1 (deadliest of all toxins), or vomitoxin (dogs and swine are most susceptible to this) that had contaminated the food. (Mycotoxins will be discussed at length in Chapter Five.) In March 1990, I sent some of the food I had to an independent lab. Within a week, the lab responded, indicating that the commercial food contained both toxins, although not in high enough levels to cause the symptoms displayed. The lab stated, "It is still possible that something is poisonous in the feed."[2]

I questioned that if it was not the mycotoxin, what else could it be? Being a health fanatic, I had read volumes on vitamins and minerals. I was aware that either one, in excess, could cause severe reactions. The fat-soluble vitamins: A, D, and E, and their toxic symptoms, were more or less ruled out. The minerals zinc, copper, and iron, in excess, would cause gastrointestinal irritation. All of these are added to commercial pet food. Since I had retained approximately half a cup of the offending food, I requested that the Ontario Ministry of Agriculture and Food, Veterinary Service Laboratory, test it for these metals.[3]

Months passed, the Ministry of Agriculture lab gave me a myriad of excuses as to why it had been unable to provide me with the results—"wrong results were sent from the lab. . .equipment broke down. . . staff went on holidays." After all these months of waiting, I learned about a reputable lab that could provide such testing. As I only had about a tablespoon of the food left, which I had kept in an air-tight bag, refrigerated, I was unsure if it was enough for testing. It was. I sent the product to another independent lab via courier. Two weeks later, I had the results. Not only had the lab provided the results for the metals I had requested (copper, zinc, and iron) but it had also found nearly twenty more metals in this pet food.[4]

The level of zinc found by the independent lab was 1,120 parts per million (ppm). I was cognizant of the fact that dogs require approximately 30 to 50 ppm of zinc in their diet but I questioned if there was a toxic level of this metal. Books acquired from the library outlined toxic levels in cows, pigs, and chickens, but no mention was made of toxic levels in companion animals. So I began the long arduous task of ascertaining if any of these metals, particularly zinc, would have caused the symptoms displayed by the dogs.

By now it was midsummer 1990 and the Ministry of Agriculture lab at Guelph had been in possession of the questionable pet food for four months and *still* had not provided any results. In my quest for information on toxic levels of heavy metals as it relates to dogs and cats, I began to contact veterinary colleges associated with universities. Along with copies of the report on mycotoxins and the report on the metals found, I sent a letter describing the symptoms, age, and breed of my dogs and the results of the tests taken by my veterinarian.

Approximately ten colleges were contacted, and most chose to respond to my query. The consensus was that "of the metals analyzed for, zinc appears to be in the toxic range. Levels of 1,000 ppm or more will result in overt toxicosis."[5] Other metals were also questioned; tungsten, calcium and phosphorus concentrations, and higher levels of iron, although toxic symptoms of these metals were different than that of zinc.[6]

Two of the doctors suggested that I contact Robert Puls, a toxicologist, who wrote the book, *Mineral Levels in Animal Health*. Puls told me that he was sure there was a similar case but could not find a record of it. He wrote, "Regardless, the analysis of your dog food leaves no doubt that a formulation mistake was made. Generally with feed formulation, errors show up as order of magnitude, as is the case with this dog food. The zinc level is ten times the amount normally added. High levels of dietary zinc are irritating to the intestinal tract, and, although I am not a veterinarian or pathologist, in my opinion the signs you describe are consistent with a diagnosis of zinc toxicity."[7]

By now, the commercial pet food company had its lawyers involved. Numerous times I had requested that the company settle this matter. The lawyers were aware that I had sent the product to three different labs for testing. By the end of 1990 they had been provided with the results I had received. The lawyers now advised me that they wanted to wait to see the report from the Ministry of Agriculture lab in Guelph. On December 5, 1990, eight months after they had been sent the pet food, the Guelph lab wrote, "We regret that we are unable to offer you the zinc and iron analyses due to maternity leave and short staffing in our laboratory. We do not expect this test will be available in the near future and therefore have not offered this test to anyone."[8] The pet food lawyers were given a copy of this letter, and again I asked that this matter be settled. I heard nothing.

On January 16, 1991, nearly one year after the incident occurred, I received the official response from the Guelph lab called the "Final Report." Not only did the mycotoxins it tested for not agree with the first lab, but its testing for zinc, iron, and copper showed completely different levels then that of the independent lab. The level of zinc found by the Guelph lab was 166 ppm as compared with the independent lab that showed zinc levels of 1,120 ppm.[9] The pet food company did not undertake any scientific lab testing of the questionable pet food.

As the commercial pet food company and its lawyers refused to settle this matter, I had no alternative but to file an action in small claims court. In Canada, as in the United States, it is not necessary to retain counsel in a small claims action—so I represented myself.

As it was not my intent to use the report from the lab in Guelph for my case against the pet food company, I did not provide its lawyers with this document. On June 6, 1991, I filed suit against one of the largest pet food companies in North America.[10] Did I intend to win? Yes. I felt confident that the documentation that I had received from the veterinary colleges would support my claim.

The pet food company filed the Canadian legal document, "Defence," and after some bureaucratic delays the trial was set for January 14, 1992.[11] Three days before the trial, a courier arrived with the evidence that the company intended to submit. This was not within the time frame required for disclosure, and I was aware that I could object if the company tried to enter it into evidence. In addition, the lawyers had enclosed a standard release form. Their client wanted to settle before this went any further. If I was willing to settle, I had to advise the lawyers so they could "call off their witnesses" before they began their journey for the trial.[12] For over two years I had requested that the company settle this case. It refused and now it was my turn to reject its offer.

The lawyers for the pet food company had to drive nearly one hundred and fifty miles. Their witnesses, the people from the Guelph lab, who had conducted the year-long test on the food, had to drive nearly one hundred miles. On January 13, weather warnings were issued. On January 14, we had a blizzard. Snow had fallen all night and high winds made it impossible to see across the road. The city was virtually closed down. Reports stated that the police were closing the highways in and out of the city. If that were the case, the lawyers and their witnesses would not make it to court.

Living within walking distance of the court, I braved the blizzard with briefcase in hand. A few lawyers drifted in and out requesting adjournments because their clients could not make it through the storm. I assumed that the pet food company lawyers would ask a local attorney to appear on their behalf to ask that this case be postponed. The bailiff approached and asked if I was the plaintiff in the pet food case. He wanted to advise me that the lawyers and their witnesses were on the highway and that the case would proceed as soon as they arrived. One hour passed, two hours passed, and finally they trooped in: two lawyers and four or five other people, snow-covered and bedraggled. Two of the people, I assumed, were the people from Guelph, but who were the others in the entourage?

The judge, an older gentleman, had to be helped to the bench. It soon became apparent that he also had a problem hearing and seeing. The learned judge, and I use the term loosely, chose not to admit as evidence the letters I had obtained from the veterinary colleges. His contention was that I had not provided copies to the lawyers two weeks prior to trial. One of the pet food company's lawyers claimed that he had not seen copies of the documents until just days before the trial. What the lawyer neglected to mention was the reason he had not seen these letters within the time frame was because he had been on vacation.

In his summation the judge stated, "After [the company] asked her to return the product, she refused and continued to feed it to the dogs knowing that it would have a detrimental effect upon them. Eventually the dogs had to be destroyed.[13] However, as far as he was concerned, there was no evidence that the dog food caused any problems. I could not believe what I was hearing. To this day I am still astounded. In one breath, the judge informs me that the dog food contained no substance that would have caused the illness but then, according to his convoluted reasoning, I persisted in feeding them the food until they were so ill they had to be destroyed.

It was eleven months after this incident that Louie died. His death was unrelated to the dog food, and I had never asserted that the pet food company was in any way responsible for his demise. As far as my dog Charlie was concerned, when I left the house at nine o'clock that morning, Charlie was alive and well.

My only consolation was that, by the time this trial was over, all roads in and out of the city were closed. The lawyers and their witnesses were forced to spend the night here.

Under no circumstance would I accept this travesty of justice. Within days I filed a motion for a new trial.[14] Filing motions is usually in the domain of lawyers but I felt competent after reading a few legal texts. The motion was filed and the date set for February 11, 1992. All parties appeared in court in February; however, it was postponed again because the judge needed to see more of the transcripts. Three judges so far and three trips back and forth for the pet food company's lawyers.

On May 14, we were all congregated in court once again. The company lawyers tried to make sure I did not get a new trial, but the judge decided a new trial should be granted, as I was barred in the previous trial from presenting evidence pertinent to the case. The objection of the lawyers was found to be unfounded. They won the first round but I had won the second round.

July 21, 1992 was the date set for the new trial. Again it was postponed as one of their "star witnesses," the witness from the Guelph lab, would be on vacation. Any time a motion was heard, any time a postponement was requested, the judge hearing such evidence had to excuse himself from hearing anything further in the case. To date, we had used *five* judges, and I began to wonder if we would run out of judges before this case was resolved. By the time the sixth court date rolled around, a judge was brought in from another city.

Finally on January 19, 1993, almost three years to the day when Louie and Charlie had become ill, the pet food company entourage filed in, consisting of the lawyers from Canada and the corporation's legal counsel from the United States. This case, a small claims action that was originally filed in the amount of $110, began to take on dimensions far beyond my original expectations.

The company presented live witnesses whom I had the opportunity to question. I had prepared the questions but I was unprepared for one of their witnesses, a doctor from the University of Saskatchewan. He was a surprise witness and was there to dispute the findings of my dogs' veterinarian.

The case lasted more than eight hours, but I did get to present all my evidence. I did get to question, at length, the people who had tested this dog food and had it in their possession for over ten months. The judge was fair. He listened intently and asked questions if he was not clear on a specific matter. Because of all the evidence admitted, and because it was well into the evening, the judge reserved his decision.

In early April, I received the Canadian court's "Reasons for Judgement."[15] I lost. There was no doubt if my witnesses had appeared in person in court (versus written correspondence) I would have had a much better chance of winning the case. However, the cost would have been astronomical for me to fly in witnesses from all over the United States and British Columbia. But that was the chance I took.

The judge asked the defendants for their formal document, "Submissions as to Costs."[16] Because it was a small claims action, recoverable costs are limited. The total claim for the pet food company was $2,378.35 for hotel accommodations, airfare allowances, service of documents, disbursements, expert testimony, and so forth, was submitted. Next, I was requested to file reasons why these costs should not be paid. Step-by-step, each issue was addressed and presented to the court. The judge decided that I should pay the defense $415. One lawyer, who sat in the court observing the process from the first to the last trial, surmised that the pet food company had spent an estimated $50,000 to defend this small claims action.

* * *

Was it worth it? Yes. Would I do it again? Yes. Because of this case, and because the pet food company chose to take the position that it was not responsible, I spent seven years learning about the pet food industry, its lack of regulations, and the inferior ingredients used in its foods. If the company had settled this matter at the onset, I would have been none the wiser.

Over the years I have received hundreds of letters from concerned pet owners convinced that something in the pet food precipitated health problems in their pets such as allergies, skin problems, cancer, aggressive behavior, and liver and kidney disease. Naturally, none of these people can prove these symptoms are caused by commercial pet food. This is what the industry counts on. Testing can be costly. Unless literally hundreds of cats and dogs become ill after ingesting a particular food, the government will not intervene.

In Canada, even if a pet food causes numerous deaths, the government cannot order the food removed from the shelves. There are no regulations. When pet owners contact the pet food company involved in their complaints, all are given the standard reply: "Send us all you have left and we will have it tested." Does this sound familiar? People comply. What alternative do they have? Within weeks, the company writes to inform the consumer that the testing showed nothing unusual. The company suggests that perhaps the pet has an allergy to an ingredient in the food or that there was some other external cause for the problem.

Never, and I emphasize, *never*, have I heard of any pet food company admitting to a complaining consumer that there may be a problem with its products. Owners are sent coupons to purchase more of the same product and an apology for any inconvenience. Many of these people are senior citizens on fixed incomes who can ill afford the high cost of veterinary bills. A number of these people have sent the pet food company involved copies of these bills. The company, claiming no fault, refuses to compensate the pet owners.

Basically, this is a self-regulated industry.

Chapter Two

Companion Animals in Pet Food

Pets in pet food? No, you say? Be assured that this is happening. Rendered companion animals are just another source of protein used in both pet food and livestock feed.

When I began investigating the ingredients used in commercial pet food, a veterinarian in the United States advised me that the use of pets in pet food was routine practice. Rendering is a cheap viable means of disposal for euthanized pets. Pets are mixed with other material from slaughterhouse facilities that have been condemned for human consumption, such as rotten meat from supermarket shelves, restaurant grease and garbage, "4-D" (dead, diseased, dying, and disabled) animals, roadkill, and even zoo animals.

John Eckhouse, a reporter for the *San Francisco Chronicle*, wrote a two-part exposé on the rendering of companion animals in California. He described how pet food companies vehemently deny that this is happening, yet a rendering industry employee confided that "it was common practice for his company to process dead pets into products sold to pet food manufacturers."[1]

To learn more about the operations of the rendering industry, I searched the shelves of the library. Perhaps because it is such a gruesome subject, nothing had been written on this topic. In early 1992, I decided to find out what was happening to the euthanized pets in the city where I live and in the surrounding area. Over the years, many of my pets have died, and I always assumed that they were either buried or cremated. I had never heard of rendering. On the death of a pet, with regard to the disposal of the body, I was told by the veterinarian, "Don't worry, we'll take care of it." Now I had to question just how they were "taking care of it."

Contacting a number of veterinary clinics in this area, I was advised that euthanized pets were being incinerated by a company that was picking them up from the clinics. After hearing the horror stories of what was happening in the United States, I was rather skeptical about Canadian practices. Without much effort I obtained the name of the company that was picking up the pets, a dead-stock removal operation. These companies pick up 4-D animals and roadkill too large to be buried roadside. Classified as "collectors," these companies, along with "receiving plants," "brokers," and "rendering plants" are licensed by the Ministry of Agriculture in Canada.

The collector picks up any dead animals (livestock) that have died or been killed in the field. The collector is also contracted by the different municipalities to pick up any large animals along the roadside. The receiving plant is where the animals are taken to be skinned and de-boned and where salable meat for animal food or pet food, is removed. A broker buys and sells this material. Rendering plants cook this material at temperatures around 250 degrees Fahrenheit.

The Canadian Ministry keeps records of the dead stock going through the system, but no records are kept on the number of companion animals, roadkill, or zoo animals processed. I asked the investigator from the ministry, "How are the dogs and cats disposed of that this company picks up?" Two months later I received a letter along with a document from the dead-stock removal company. This document, addressed to the investigator, was stamped that the information contained in this specific document was "not to be made known to any other agency or person without the written permission of the Chief Investigator."[2]

It was clear why the dead-stock removal company did not want this information released. The contents of the document described how the pets were being disposed of by this facility. Unless it was "specially requested," and "paid to be cremated by their owners or by the veterinary clinic," these animals were being disposed of by rendering. I checked back with the veterinarians, and found that none of them were paying extra to have animals cremated. The standard fee (from $20 up, depending on the size of the animal) was for the disposal of the animal and the fee did not include cremation.

The document noted where these animals were being shipped—to a broker located about three hundred miles away. Again I contacted the government investigator for this particular area and asked what happened to the animals when they reached this point. The investigator promptly replied.[3] The facility was just a stopping point for these animals. The gentleman is a broker. His job is to find a renderer that pays the highest price for this material. The investigator was kind enough to advise me what rendering plant the broker was selling to at that time. The plant was located in another province, Quebec.

My next step was to contact the rendering plant in Quebec. (As I am not versed in French, this became a hardship.) The first question I asked was: "Are cats and dogs rendered with other material such as livestock, roadkill, etcetera?" The owner's reply was, "Yes." I went on to ask: "Do pet food companies purchase this rendered material?" Again his reply was, "Yes." "Could he please advise me what other sources might use this rendered material?" "Mill Plant," he replied. Mill Plant is a facility that makes and sells livestock feed.[4]

The path of the euthanized pet went from the veterinary clinic to the receiving plant, then to the broker, and finally to the rendering plant where it was rendered and sold to feed mills and pet food companies. Most of these pets travel further in death than they did in life. I was numb. *How had this barbaric practice gone undetected all these years?* These were not the Dark Ages, this was the 1990s. The feeding of companion animals to our pet is a source of protein yes, but as this book will explain, a dangerous one. And personally, I found this aesthetically disgusting.

Still not believing what I was hearing and reading, I contacted the Minister of Agriculture in Quebec. I asked that he confirm that this practice was actually happening. In broken English, the minister wrote, "Dead animals are cooked together with viscera, bones and fats at 115 degrees Celsius (C.) [230 degrees Fahrenheit (F.)] for twenty minutes." Also, "The fur is not removed from dogs and cats."[5] In later investigations in both the United States and Canada, I was to learn that the collars, tags, flea collars, and even the plastic bags in which the pets are wrapped, are not removed before they are shoved into the rendering pit. Deceased pets were and are being "recycled" into pet food, and pet owners have no knowledge as to what is happening.

When I advised the veterinarians in my city about what was happening to the carcasses, most of them immediately ceased using this dead-stock company and began using the local humane society where the animals are cremated. (The cost to cremate is the same amount paid to the dead-stock company, so the vets did not lose any money.) I had to question that if this was happening in our city, how many other cities, provinces, and states condoned this means of disposal? How many owners would be abhorred if they knew?

In the United States and Canada, the rendering of companion animals is not illegal, and literally millions of pets are disposed of by this method each year. According to the *San Francisco Chronicle* article, an employee and ex-employee of a rendering plant in California stated that their company "rendered somewhere between 10,000 and 30,000 pounds of dogs and cats a day out of a total of 250,000 to 500,000 pounds of cattle, poultry, butcher shop scraps and other material." These employees were well aware that the finished product was being used by the pet food industry.

A March 1997 article in *The New York Times* stated:

> Renderers in the United States pick up one hundred million pounds of waste material every day—a witch's brew of feet, heads, stomachs, intestines, hooves, spinal cords, tails, grease, feathers and bones....An estimated six million to seven million dogs and cats are killed in animal shelters each year, said Jeff Frace, a spokesman for the American Society for the Prevention of Cruelty to Animals in New York City.
>
> For example, the city of Los Angeles sends two hundred tons of euthanized cats and dogs to West Coast Rendering, in Los Angeles, every month, according to Chuck Ellis, a spokesman for the city's Sanitation Department.
>
> Pet food companies try not to buy meat and bone meal from renderers who grind up cats and dogs, said Doug Anderson, president of Darling International, Inc., a large rendering company in Dallas. "We do not accept companion animals," he said. "But there are still a number of small plants that will render anything."[6]

In Canada, the rendering plant in Quebec was rendering eleven tons of dogs and cats per week. This is from one province alone. When I called the owner of a pet food company located in this area, I asked if its meat meal contained companion animals. An emphatic "No," was the reply. "What made up the meat meal?" I asked. "Beef and other meal but no dogs or cats," the company owner replied. When I asked if he would disclose the name of the plant where he purchased the rendered material, he said he could not remember. He would have to look it up and call me back. "Give me an hour or so," he responded. I never heard from him again.

In the intervening years, I have faxed rendering plants numerous times both in this province and in Quebec to ask, "Do you render companion animals?" One plant replied that it prohibits dogs and cats from being included in its material.[7] None of the other eight plants have chosen to reply, even though I have faxed each one of them at least five times. The continued lack of response leads me to believe that they have something to hide.

My next venture was to find a laboratory that could test pet food in order to ascertain the sources of protein. This did not seem like an insurmountable task. Approximately ten laboratories were contacted but none had the resources to test for the sources of protein. They could determine the level of protein, but not the source. I was told that if such testing was available, it would be cost-prohibitive to undertake.

When I determined that companion animals were being rendered and used in these foods, I contacted our provincial minister of agriculture, the Honorable Elmer Buchanan, and asked if he was aware of what was happening. He replied that none of the rendering plants were rendering pets; therefore, none of the pet food companies could be using this material in their products however, the people in his department, the investigators, were the very people who had provided me with the documentation showing where the pets from this area were going.

If this was the case in Canada, I wondered, *Was the United States government aware of what was happening?* So I queried them. The U.S. Department of Agriculture/Food Safety and Inspection Services (USDA/FSIS), wrote, "Federal meat and poultry regulations also provide FSIS the authority to provide special inspection services to pet food manufacturers that choose to include meat and poultry products that have been inspected and passed, and so marked, in their product. Such services [which is available to any pet food company] enable pet food manufacturers to produce products that are classified and labeled as 'Packed Under Continuous Inspection of U.S. Department of Agriculture.'"[8]

The code states that dog and cat cadavers are excluded as an ingredient in pet food under this regulation. Labeling, as such, provides the consumer with specific knowledge that dogs and cats are not in the food. The other ingredients that are in these foods is questionable. Nonetheless, it seemed a step in the right direction. I asked the USDA if it could provide me with a list of the companies that were using this inspection service. The reply from the USDA was that two small facilities were licensed for this service but that neither had subscribed to said service for four years.[9]

Many pet food companies advertise that only *quality* meats are being used in their products. However, as of 1996 not one of the pet food companies was using the inspection service offered by the USDA. As a concerned consumer and pet owner, I would want to know about the sources of protein used in pet food. As a conscientious consumer, I would want a food that was inspected by the USDA and guaranteed not to contain any diseased material or remains of dogs and cats. This response led me to ask, *Why would none of these multinationals use the services provided by the USDA?*

The Food and Drug Administration/Center for Veterinary Medicine (FDA/CVM) responded to my query regarding the disposal of pets: "In recognizing the need for disposal of a large number of unwanted pets in this country, CVM has not acted to specifically prohibit the rendering of pets. However, that is not to say that the practice of using this material in pet food is condoned by CVM."[10] Not condoned, but apparently no steps have been taken to eliminate or restrict this practice. Apparently the FDA believes that the proportion of dogs and cats rendered is small in comparison to the number of livestock sent to these facilities.

One veterinarian associated with a large U.S. veterinary clinic stated that other than the aesthetic aspect, nothing was objectionable about cats and dogs ingesting material that contained their kind. With the information that has come to light, I am not in agreement with this doctor. Finding companion pets eating dead cats and dogs objectionable is more than just aesthetics. Safety is at stake.

Sodium pentobarbital, a barbiturate, used to euthanize companion animals and in some cases, livestock and horses, should not be used on animals intended for food. The 1993 "Report of the American Veterinary Medical Association (AVMA) Panel on Euthanasia," states:

> In euthanasia of animals intended for human or animal food, agents that result in tissue residues cannot be used unless they are approved by the U.S. Food and Drug Administration. Carbon dioxide is the only chemical currently used in euthanasia of food animals that does not lead to tissue residues. Carcasses of animals euthanized by barbituric acid derivatives or other chemical agents may contain potentially harmful residues. These carcasses should be disposed of in a manner that will prevent them from being consumed by human beings or animals.[11]

In a study conducted at the University of Minnesota, it was noted that the barbiturate sodium pentobarbital "survived rendering without undergoing degradation."[12] The study points to one case in which a dog exhibited pentobarbital toxicosis after eating the thoracic organs of a calf. The levels of pentobarbital had not decreased in the kidney of the calf after boiling for twenty minutes. In contacting two pharmaceutical companies, one in the United States and one in Canada, who make this drug, I queried as to the heat lability (the temperature at which the drug begins to degrade). The first company, in Canada, faxed me a copy of the "Compendium of Veterinary Products,"[13] which referred to sodium pentobarbital. This information provided no insight into the degradation of this drug and I was advised that any other information on this substance was of a "proprietary nature." The firm in the United States did not reply. To date there is no way to determine what effect this drug might have on pets ingesting foods contaminated with sodium pentobarbital. This is what I concluded in regards to sodium pentobarbital:

- ♦ Pets and some livestock and horses are euthanized with sodium pentobarbital;
- ♦ These animals are rendered;
- ♦ Rendering does not break down sodium pentobarbital;
- ♦ This rendered material is being used in pet food and livestock feed.

Universities, veterinary colleges, and researchers in the United States and Canada, to my knowledge, have not undertaken any type of testing in order to ascertain the level of sodium pentobarbital found in pet food and livestock feed. Laboratories in the United States told me that if I could even find a lab willing to undertake testing for this drug, the cost would run from $300 to $400 per sample. However, even if the barbiturate was not found in one sample, the next sample—made by the same company, containing the same ingredients—could very well contain the drug. Seldom does each batch contain the same material as another. I contacted a dozen labs in both the United States and Canada and could not find a laboratory in either country that can undertake testing to determine the level of sodium pentobarbital in pet food and livestock feed.

The Association of American Feed Control Officials (AAFCO) states that there are no restrictions limiting the use of animals for meat meal, tankage, and digest. AAFCO does not prohibit rendered companion animals in pet foods or livestock feed—it is a source of protein.

In early 1995, I sent a questionnaire to each state in the United States. One question I asked was, "Does your state prohibit the use of rendered companion animals in pet foods?" The states that chose to reply and their comments regarding the use of pets in pet foods, are as follows:

ALASKA:	No regulations at all. Anything can be used in pet food.[14]
ALABAMA:	No stipulation as to the sources of protein which can be used in meat meals, tankage and digests.[15]
ARIZONA:	Did not answer this question.[16]
FLORIDA:	No regulations on pet food.[17]
GEORGIA:	Do not prohibit the use of companion animals.[18]
IDAHO:	Do not test as to the sources of protein.[19]
ILLINOIS:	Do not specifically prohibit the use of pets. Ingredients have to be cleared with the FDA before being accepted by this state.[20]
INDIANA:	Do not prohibit the use of companion animals in pet foods or livestock feed.[21]
KENTUCKY:	Although they do not test for the sources of proteins which are used, they state, "Official definitions for rendered products establishes which species of animal is acceptable to render." They neglect to mention which species of animal is acceptable.[22]
MASSACHUSETTS:	Did not answer this question.[23]

MISSOURI:	Do not prohibit dogs and cats from being used in pet food.[24]
NEW JERSEY:	Do not prohibit companion animals in pet food.[25]
NEW YORK:	Does not prohibit the use of rendered companion animals.[26]
NORTH CAROLINA:	They replied that the use of companion animals is not acceptable in their state but apparently do not prohibit the use of such animals.[27]
OHIO:	Did not to respond to this question.[28]
OKLAHOMA:	Not aware of any state dog food processors that used companion animals in their food.[29]
OREGON:	No testing as to sources of protein.[30]
RHODE ISLAND:	Did not answer this question.[31]
SOUTH CAROLINA:	Advised that I contact another agency regarding this question. No reply yet.[32]
WYOMING:	Do not prohibit the use of rendered companion animals in pet food.[33]

States That Did Not Reply:

ARKANSAS	MARYLAND	PENNSYLVANIA
CALIFORNIA	MICHIGAN	SOUTH DAKOTA
COLORADO	MINNESOTA	TENNESSEE
CONNECTICUT	MISSISSIPPI	TEXAS
DELAWARE	MONTANA	UTAH
HAWAII	NEBRASKA	VERMONT
IOWA	NEVADA	VIRGINIA
KANSAS	NEW HAMPSHIRE	WASHINGTON
LOUISIANA	NEW MEXICO	WEST VIRGINIA
MAINE	NORTH DAKOTA	WISCONSIN

Among the states that did not reply is California, which was contacted twice. California was of interest because it had enacted the "Pure Pet Food Act" in 1969. Unaware of the terminology of this act, I faxed the Department of Health Services in February of 1996. I asked, "Did this act ban the use of companion animals in pet foods manufactured in California?" The reply I received was that the code "dealing with Processed Pet Food, defines, 'Meat' as clean wholesome flesh derived from slaughtered mammals. Therefore, in answer to your inquiry about the inclusion of euthanized companion animals, such animals are not allowed in pet food manufactured in California in that they do not die by slaughter."[34]

The mistake I had made was that I had not been specific in asking about meat meal, digests, and tankage and if this material contained pets. (I often chide my friends that when they require information, especially from government agencies, to be specific.) Another letter was sent to the Department of Health Services asking if it could provide the composition of meats, etcetera. My question was, "Could you please advise the composition of meat meal used in commercial pet foods in California?" I received no reply. Again I contacted them and as of press time I had not received a reply.

As I had not been in contact with the Ministry of Agriculture in Quebec for more than three years, I wanted to ascertain if its practice of rendering pets continued. The 1996 communiqué from Michel Houle, Inspector of Agriculture and Fisheries, stated, "In Quebec, the recovery of companion animals for the rendering of unfit meat is permitted."[35] Dogs and cats are still being supplied to these facilities.

In September 1995, an article appeared in the Baltimore *City Paper* by journalist Van Smith entitled, "Meltdown." It describes what happens at a rendering plant. This article, replete with pictures, shows barrels of dead dogs and cats about to be rendered. Smith describes how carcasses from zoo animals and "thousands of dead dogs, cats, raccoons, possums, deer, foxes, snakes, and the rest that local animal shelters and roadkill patrols must dispose of each month" are rendered. "In a gruesomely ironic twist, most inedible dead animal parts, including dead pets, end up in feed used to fatten future generations of their kind."[36]

Once you sign the authorization paper for the euthanization and subsequent disposal of your pet, you basically have no say as to how the animal is disposed of. In some communities, pets can be buried on private property in accordance with city regulations. You can also pay a fee and have a private cremation with the ashes returned to you, but even this is questionable. A friend recently had a German Shepherd cremated. Her friend had a much smaller dog cremated at the same time. Upon the return of the ashes the friends found that the small dog resulted in more ashes returned than that of the shepherd.

Most of the fifty U.S. and Canadian veterinarians with whom I have spoken claim to have no knowledge of rendering as a means of disposal. Veterinarians also claim to have no knowledge of the fact that these rendered companion animals along with their collars, tags, and flea collars, are being processed and finding their way into commercial pet food. Ironically, some veterinarians often recommend these same commercial pet foods, and, in some cases, even sell them.

Government and voluntary organizations do not have a set program to test commercial pet food. We mistakenly rely on the pet food industry, an industry that assures us that companion animals are not included in pet food ingredient lists. Questions I wanted answered by the pet food industry included: *Do pet food companies conduct any testing to see if this is the case? Are there any DNA markers for dogs and cats? Do pet food companies have the methodology to detect sodium pentobarbital?* From the five Canadian and the eight U.S. pet food companies I spoke to, no testing is conducted that would indicate the composition of the material purchased from rendering plants. No DNA markers are yet available and none has the means to detect barbiturates.

It is apparent that federal and provincial governments in Canada are aware of these practices. The state and federal agencies in the United States are also cognizant of this lack of regulation—and it continues. Their reasoning for this means of disposal is that the landfill sites cannot accept any more waste, so we must recycle. Incineration is not environmentally friendly. But then what about rendering plants? In this day and age most older incinerators are being brought up to code. New incinerators are clean and nonpolluting and meet or exceed the standards that are set by the Ministry of the Environment.

Construction of incinerators can be a costly venture, but they are clearly a more viable means for the disposal of pets. Perhaps the industries that purport to care about the health and welfare of our pets, the industries that stand to profit the most from our pets—the pet food companies—could contribute a percentage of their advertising dollars to erect such facilities.

Chapter Three

Mad Cow Disease and How It Relates to Our Pets

In recent years, the public has become aware of mad cow disease, also known as bovine spongiform encephalopathy (BSE). In 1985 the first cases of BSE began to emerge in the United Kingdom. By 1990 there were at least 15,000 confirmed cases and by 1996 the number had risen to 150,000.[1] Creutzfeldt-Jakob disease (CJD) is the human form of spongiform encephalopathy. CJD is a progressive and invariably fatal dementia. Humans developing this disease deteriorate quickly. The British government denied that mad cow disease and Creutzfeldt-Jakob disease occurring in a younger population had any connection.[2] They were wrong.

In 1990 in England, a Siamese cat called Max died of an unknown spongiform encephalopathy. Zoo animals in England (antelope, cheetahs and ostriches) began dropping dead from ingesting contaminated meat products from British cattle. Where did this disease in cattle originate?

The suspected cause came from sheep infected with ovine spongiform encephalopathy, or scrapie. Scrapie is a disease in which sheep suffer from severe itching to the point where the sheep actually scrape off their hair and wool. These spongiform encephalopathies, scrapies, mad cow disease, and CJD are all caused by prions. Stanley Prusiner, Ph.D., discovered prions in the 1970s. Prions are neither a virus nor bacteria. Prions are an infectious protein without detectable DNA or RNA. They cannot be destroyed by cooking or freezing. Ionizing, radiation, autoclaving, sterilization, bleach, and formaldehyde have little effect on them. Prions are infectious proteins that can live in soil for years.[3]

Michael Greger, who undertook extensive research in this area, presented an in-depth paper at the 1996 World Vegetarian Congress on BSE called "The Public Health Implications of Mad Cow Disease." In his research paper he stated, "Prions are called the most intriguing, unsolved puzzle in modern biology. The whole concept of prions challenges the basic tenet of biology. Prions have also been called the strangest thing in all biology. It is not known how they replicate and because of their unique makeup, they are practically invulnerable."[4]

In the United Kingdom, sheep infected with scrapie were rendered and this material was fed back to cattle and processed into pet food. Rendering temperatures do not eradicate these prions. This is the suspected route of death for Max the cat back in 1990.

Scrapie was first noted in U.S. sheep in 1947 and sheep infected with this disease exist in almost every state in the United States.[5] The rendering of sheep and cattle into livestock feed and pet food transmitted this disease to cows. After the deaths of a number of young people in Great Britain from CJD, a disease that typically affects people in their sixties and seventies, a worldwide ban was imposed on British beef. Prior to the imposition of this ban in 1989, approximately 499 cattle had been imported to the United States, some during the height of the BSE epidemic. Of those cattle, 188 head were sent to rendering, apparently to be fed back to livestock and processed into pet food. And thirty-four of these cattle have not been traced.[6] Between 1982 and 1992, thirteen tons of meat and bone meat implicated in the birth of the British epidemic entered the United States from England.[7]

With the implication that BSE cattle had been instrumental in causing the early deaths of at least ten young people who had contracted CJD, both U.S. and Canadian governments became concerned. One case, a cow imported from the United Kingdom and infected with BSE, was found in Canada. In April 1996, elk from a game farm near Regina, Saskatchewan was also found to have transmissible spongiform encephalopathy (TSE). According to the *London Free Press*, zoo animals mainly in the United Kingdom, such as puma, cheetah, ocelot, nyala, eland, Arabian oryx, kudu, have also contracted TSE from eating rendered material.[8] There are at least two documented cases of this disease in Canada. Both the FDA and USDA state that no cases of this disease are present in the United States.

Since 1947 there have been twenty-five outbreaks of mink spongiform encephalopathy in the United States. This perplexed researchers who had been unable to orally infect mink with TME using scrapie infected sheep brains.[9] A clue came in 1985 when TSE wiped out more than seven thousand mink at a mink ranch in Wisconsin. These animals were fed almost exclusively on dairy cows called "downers." The United States Department of Agriculture describes "downers" as a meat and dairy industries term that defines factory farm animals that have fallen and die each year from "unexplainable" (sic) causes.[10] (People in animal reform attribute the cause for downed animals to the inhumane treatment of animals raised on factory farms and stressful procedures when transporting the animals for slaughter.) It has been estimated that about 300,000 farm animals each year are classified as downers.

When University of Wisconsin veterinary scientist Richard Marsh, inoculated U.S. cattle with the infected mink brains, the cattle died. When Marsh fed the brains of these cows to healthy mink, they also died of a spongiform encephalopathy. Dr. Marsh theorized that an indigenous U.S. strain of BSE already existed and that it manifests itself as a "downer cow" disease rather than as "mad cow" disease as found in the United Kingdom.[11]

Seven thousand mink died at this ranch in Wisconsin and apparently no one has ever questioned how these animals were disposed of. The cattle injected with the infected mink brains also died. How were *they* disposed of? These are two important questions that no one has delved into. The U.S. government continues to deny that this disease exists in the United States, but unless these mink and cattle were incinerated, it does exist.

At the time of the experiments undertaken by Dr. Marsh in 1985, the prion theory was just that, a *theory*. It was not until approximately two years later, although found in the 1970s, that prions were connected to BSE or any of the TSE diseases. As was mentioned, the British government assumed that rendering would destroy this disease.

My queries regarding how the mink and cattle in the United States were disposed of began with the Food and Drug Administration/Center for Veterinary Medicine (FDA/CVM). The questions I asked included, "Were these animals buried, incinerated, or rendered?" The FDA/CVM did not reply. My next letter was directed to Dr. Marsh who had performed the mink-to-cattle experiments. No reply was received from Dr.

Marsh. (Dr. Marsh died in March 1997.) My final query was posed to another doctor with the FDA. No reply. I contacted researcher Michael Greger who, as I mentioned earlier, had written an extensive paper, "The Public Health Implications of Mad Cow Disease" but he had no details on the seven thousand mink or the cattle.

In early 1997, I contacted a person who works for the USDA (and who has requested anonymity) on a matter unrelated to the mink and cattle situation. Realizing that this person would have knowledge in this area, I questioned if he was aware of how the cattle and mink were disposed of. The reply was, "I'd have to check my references for the results of Marsh's work, but it is my understanding that the mink were rendered and fed back to other mink and the cattle involved in the research were similarly disposed of."[12] Were these cattle rendered and fed back to other cattle? One teaspoon of BSE-contaminated food, according to the Physicians Committee for Responsible Medicine, can transmit the disease to other animals.[13]

As of 1996 approximately three thousand brains of U.S. cattle have been examined at USDA labs located throughout the country. That makes about one in every 30,000 animals arriving at slaughter. Brains from these cattle were examined for signs of BSE.[14] Animal and Plant Health Inspection Services, the agency that oversees the health of live-stock, states that the possibility of BSE appearing in U.S. cattle is extremely remote. However, the incubation period is three to five years before any overt clinical signs of BSE would emerge. Cattle are usually slaughtered before any signs of BSE would be recognized. Approx-imately 46 percent of U.S. dairy cattle live to four years of age or older compared to 70 percent of dairy cows in the United Kingdom.[15]

In August 1994, the FDA issued a "proposed" rule declaring that specified offal from adult sheep and goats (goats also get scrapie), are generally not recognized as safe for use in ruminant feed. The specified offal includes tissue from the brain, spinal cord, spleen, thymus, ton-sils, lymph nodes, and intestines.[16] The dead-stock operations and ren-dering plants were asked not to pick up or render sheep or goats, as they might be carriers of scrapie. Shortly after the United States announced their "voluntary ban," Canada followed. In 1993 the USDA published a survey in which they found that 71 percent of renderers were still combining sheep offal with that of other species.[17] It is doubtful that this number has decreased. Rendering is the cheapest means of disposal. Voluntary bans usually do not work.

In a fax from Agriculture Canada, July 1996, I was advised, "At the present time there is no federal legislation that prohibits the rendering of sheep." Further, "Rendered sheep may be sold as livestock feed or to the pet food industry." Without proper legislation, without proper enforcement, the rendering of sheep and goats will continue.[18]

In April of 1996, Howard Lyman from The Humane Society of the United States (HSUS) and Gary Weber, DVM, Director of Beef Safety and Cattle Health for the National Cattleman's Beef Association (NCBA) appeared on the "Oprah Winfrey Show." The topic of the discussion on that day was mad cow disease and the implications it has had on the British beef industry and the consumers in the United Kingdom. Dr. Weber advised the audience that government regulations have seen to it that the U.S. beef supply is safe and that the U.S. has not imported any beef into this country since 1985. Howard Lyman, a former cattle rancher turned vegetarian, disagreed. Lyman discussed the number of 4-D animals that are rendered and fed back to other animals. When Winfrey asked Lyman how he knew cows were ground up and fed back to other cows, Lyman stated that there are USDA statistics to back up his statements. Weber countered, and the discussion continued.[19]

After this television show aired, cattle prices plummeted in the United States. Oprah Winfrey invited Dr. Weber back to the show to dispute some of the statements made by Howard Lyman. On a second appearance, Dr. Weber reiterated his position on BSE and cattle eating cattle. He also stated that due to concerns regarding feeding ruminants-to-ruminants, this practice would no longer continue.

Regarding the aftermath of the television show, *Earth Island Journal* reported the following:

> **Nine days after Howard Lyman's appearance on the "Oprah Winfrey Show," Texas Agriculture Commissioner Rick Perry asked Attorney General Dan Morales to take legal action against Lyman for saying that Mad Cow Disease would "make AIDS look like the common cold" and claiming that ranchers feed "roadkill" to cattle.[20]**

The suit was filed under the Food Disparagement Act of 1991. As of press time, thirteen states have enacted the act, and eight state legislatures have bills pending. Although the laws vary somewhat, the act gives food producers a cause of action against those who make "disparaging statements" and disseminate "false information" about the safety of the their products.[21] The act was generated by agriculture, chemical, and biotechnology lobbyists. Other states are considering adopting the Food Disparagement Act.[22] Serious questions of constitutionality have arisen over the enactment of this law as an infringement of the First Amendment to the Constitution—the basic right of freedom of speech.

In early May 1996, after the "Oprah Winfrey Show" on mad cow disease, I contacted the FDA/CVM for documentation that ruminants would no longer be rendered and fed back to other animals. I wanted to know, "Were these government-enforced regulations?" In mid-May I received a fax from the FDA/CVM stating, "At this stage, we are looking only at ruminant-to-ruminant. Thus, it would not affect feeding of non-ruminant-to ruminant or ruminant-to-non-ruminant."[23] In other words, rendered cattle, sheep, goats, mule deer, and elk would no longer be fed to the same. Roadkill, euthanized dogs and cats, zoo animals, and anything else non-ruminant could still be fed to livestock. Rendered cattle, sheep, goats, mule deer, and elk could still be fed to chickens, turkeys, cats, and dogs.

If the disease is present in cattle in the United States, BSE may manifest itself in a different way than the cattle in the United Kingdom. In England, presumably scrapie-infected cows go mad, twitching and kicking into a rabid frenzy. But in the United States, scrapie-infected cows instead stagger to their deaths."[24]

Numerous tests have been conducted and none of these tests exclude the possibility that U.S. cattle harbor some form of BSE. The USDA looked for the British strain of BSE, disregarding the evidence as found by Dr. Marsh relating to the mink-to-cattle research. In 1992 a panel comprised of the National Milk Producers Federation, the National Renderers Association, the National Cattlemen's Association, and the American Sheep Industry Association, decided that "changes in the research program to accommodate the possibility that BSE was already present in the United States were not appropriate at this time.'" It was felt by this panel that because no cases had been reported in the United States, that no program was necessary. Journalists closely eyeing this situation cannot help but ask what the impact would be on the beef industry if BSE was discovered in the U.S. cattle. An *In These*

Times article asserted, "The USDA knows all too well that a positive diagnosis in a single cow could put the entire dairy and beef export business in jeopardy."[25]

These special associations and government agencies are asking consumers to trust them. Basically, the British government did the same thing in the early 1980s. Britain's Meat and Livestock Commission countered gathering fears with a £6.5 million advertising campaign touting red-meat consumption. Television spots featured the Minister of Agriculture exclaiming, "It's delicious!" while eating burgers with his four-year old daughter Cordelia.[26] Public relations campaigns launched by the British Meat and Livestock Commission touted the virtues of red meat.

However, young people started dying of Creutzfeldt-Jakob disease. CJD spontaneously strikes one in a million people with the average age of sixty-seven.[27] This new strain was killing people as young as twenty years. The Physicians Committee for Responsible Medicine, based in Washington, D.C. reports, "The cases receiving most recent attention in the United Kingdom are those of young people (ten cases so far) and dairy farmers (four so far), all of whom have eaten beef products in the preceding ten years, although one later became a vegetarian in 1991."[28]

The World Health Organization agreed with the British government's assessment linking the disease in people with the disease in cows. The British government finally realized that the public needed to know the facts.

These diseases, BSE, TSE, and CJD, can be transmitted from sheep to cattle, from cattle to other ruminants and non-ruminants, and from cattle to humans. Where do pets fit into this picture? As of July 1997, more than one hundred cats in the United Kingdom have died of feline spongiform encephalopathy (FSE). Many believe this is from the cats eating cat food contaminated with rendered animals that have died from mad cow disease or any other animals that may have carried this disease. As of mid-1997, no cases of dogs developing a canine form of this disease have been documented. Is that because the incubation period is longer in dogs? Are they dying of other causes before this disease can be diagnosed? Are dogs somehow immune from this disease? BSE in cattle manifests as apprehension, poor coordination, difficulties in walking and weight loss, and degenerative disease affecting the central nervous system. Neurological disease in dogs can manifest itself in much the same way. The infections that cause BSE apparently can exist for several years before the disease is recognized.[29]

The only way to ascertain if this condition exists is by a brain autopsy. The question I have posed to numerous veterinarians is, "If a dog was brought to you displaying neurological disease, what is standard procedure?" The first step is to ascertain rabies. Ruling rabies out, the next step would be to see if an identifiable toxin was the cause. Unless the specific toxin is known, it would, in most cases, be cost-prohibitive to test for every imaginable toxin. Old age in a pet plays a part in neurological disease. Pets suffering diseases of unknown origin are usually euthanized.

I also asked, "Do the owner's usually request an autopsy to ascertain the cause?" Veterinarian Richard Pitcairn stated, "Very, very few owners would request a complete autopsy on a pet dead from neurological disease. To do this properly, the skull must be opened, and I never encountered a practitioner prepared to do this."[30] I had mentioned to Dr. Pitcairn that the FDA/CVM advised that no cases of either BSE or TSE existed in the United States. Dr. Pitcairn replied, "If they do not test or evaluate, how can they know of incidents?"

The question of a misdiagnosis of a sick dog still haunted me. Scott McEwen, DVM, at the University of Guelph, Veterinary College, provided further insight into this mystery. "It is technically impractical to examine the entire brain histologically. Obviously, if the disease has not been described in dogs, the location of lesions in the brain of a dog is also unknown."[31] From this statement I have to surmise that even if brain autopsies (necropsies in veterinary parlance) were conducted, pathologists would not be aware of these lesions if they did exist.

Andrew Mackin, professor at the Royal School of Veterinary Studies at the University of Edinburgh, Scotland, does not believe BSE exists in dogs. "If the condition did occur in dogs, then it is highly likely that they would also succumb...in which case, it is most surprising that no veterinary pathologist to date, anywhere, has to my knowledge, reported the disease in dogs or found it on post-mortem." He goes on to write in personal correspondence to me, "Still...we can never say with absolute certainty. Maybe one day someone will report a dog with a BSE-like disease."[32]

Are dogs dying from other diseases before the outward signs of the canine form of BSE appear? Are dogs immune from this disease and if such immunity exists, why has it not been investigated? Dogs and cats eat the same rendered material, and many cats have died from the feline form of BSE but no dogs. Government agencies state that dogs are not and have never been infected with the canine form of BSE.

On April 22, 1997, the Associated Press reported:

Dog lovers in Norway are nervous over reports that a gold retriever's death looks similar to mad-cow disease. Norway's TV2 reported that an autopsy of the eleven-year old dog showed changes in the brain consistent with those seen in the brains of cows who die of the disease. If the dog contracted the brain ailment, it probably was through dog food in the late 1980s, national animal health board director Eivind Liven told the national news agency.[33]

In April 1997, the British newspaper, *The Daily Telegraph*, reported:

Tests six years ago by ministry experts on the brains of 444 hunting hounds found some abnormalities called fibrils. However, some brains had started to degenerate making the results ambiguous.

The results were passed to the Spongiform Encephalopathy Advisory Committee, which agreed that they were inconclusive and ruled out further research because there was no public health issue. "We don't eat dogs in Britain," the spokesman said.[34]

Veterinarians in private practice admit that this disease could be misdiagnosed as no one seems to know where to look for the lesions in the brain. Until scientific data is presented, actually showing the area of the brain and the description of this disease in dogs, we will have to assume that dogs are not at risk. However, rendered animal remains are the mainstay of the pet food industry. Rendered sheep, goats, and rendered offal from cattle, brains, spinal cords, tonsils, lymph nodes, etcetera—all are suspect of causing BSE and TSE.

Should we be concerned that there may be contamination of pet food with one of these spongiform encephalopathies? Is the pet food industry concerned? *Petfood Industry* magazine states, "The Pet Food Institute and its members will continue to monitor actions of the U.S. government and the beef supply and other pet food ingredients and provide relevant information to pet owners."[35] It further assures its readers that no beef cattle have been imported from the United Kingdom since 1989. However, what was not noted in the article is that by 1989 BSE was well established in the United Kingdom and cattle, meat, and bone meal from the United Kingdom had already made its way into the United States.

The lamb and rice foods that most veterinarians recommend if a pet has a suspected allergy are very suspect. The estimation is that 4,500 pounds per day of sheep are rendered. This would produce five tons of the lamb and rice foods. Because dogs have not displayed any symptoms of BSE, or so the FDA/CVM tells us, the use of rendered sheep in dog food is acceptable. Because this disease has been diagnosed in cats it has been suggested, by the industry, that lamb meal be obtained from countries that have no scrapie infection in sheep.[36]

This is a serious concern. If sheep with scrapie are being rendered, (and remember in the United Kingdom the rendered sheep with scrapie caused mad cow disease) and fed back to dogs, these dogs are then rendered and fed back to livestock and processed into pet food. The circle continues.

"Don't worry, don't panic," the USDA and other government agencies tell us, "the meat supply is safe." Would the government cover up the fact that BSE exists? Other countries that have far less to lose, have suppressed information on BSE. Greger states in his research paper, "In Germany, for example, scientists have admitted that many cases of BSE were not reported." According to the Physicians Committee for Responsible Medicine, "Ireland also reportedly concealed a recent BSE outbreak to protect exports." It has been reported that cases of BSE in the United Kingdom have been "severely under-reported."[37] Would the Canadian and the United States governments cover up? The rendering of euthanized companion animals right here in the Canadian province where I reside is a good example. The Minister of Agriculture vehemently denied that this was happening, yet his very own staff was providing the documentation that showed otherwise.

Other groups are asking questions. The Physicians Committee for Responsible Medicine has made some valid points:

1. The conditions that lead to the emergence of BSE in Britain are present in the United States. Current U.S. livestock rendering and feeding practices are similar to those present in the Britain at the onset of the BSE epidemic;

2. Evidence suggests that the agent that causes BSE has already spread to at least some animals in the United States;

3. Between 1979 and 1980, 2,614 Americans died of Creutzfeldt-Jakob disease, and the possibility that BSE played a role in some of those deaths cannot be ruled out.[38]

An article written in 1996 by John Stauber and Sheldon Rampton for *Earth Island Journal*, "The U.S. 'Mad Cow' Cover-Up," states:

> Internal documents and PR plans obtained by PR Watch, via a Freedom of Information Act investigation, show that the U.S. government has sought to protect the economic interest of the powerful meat and animal feed industries (this includes pet foods), while denying the existence of risks to animal and human health...In an 1991 internal PR document, the USDA advised officials to use the technical name for the disease. "The term 'Mad Cow Disease' has been detrimental" the document explained. "We should emphasize the need to use the term 'bovine spongiform encephalopathy' or 'BSE.'"[39]

After seven years of research, I believe that BSE exists in the United States and Canada and that in the near future, despite denials by the two governments, we will find ourselves in a similar situation as the United Kingdom. Is the health and welfare of our pets at risk? Yes, not only from the inferior ingredients, but from this new, deadly threat, BSE. Humans are not directly eating the brains, spinal cords, and other remnants of cows, but our pets are. If this disease exists our pets will surely suffer the consequences.

Chapter Four

Sources of Meat, Carbohydrates, and Fiber

Television commercials and magazine advertisements for pet food would have us believe that the meats, grains, and fats used in these foods could grace our own dining tables. Chicken, beef, lamb, whole grains, and quality fats are supposedly the composition of dog and cat food.

In my opinion, when we purchase these bags and cans of commercial food, we are in most cases purchasing garbage. Unequivocally, I cannot state that all pet food falls into this category, but I have yet to find one that I could, in all good conscience, feed my dog or cats.

Pet food labels can be deceiving. They only provide half the story. The other half of the story is hidden behind obscure ingredients listed on the labels. Bit by bit, over seven years, I have been able to unearth information about *what* is contained in most commercial pet food. At first I was shocked, but my shock turned to anger when I realized how little the consumer is told about the actual contents of the pet food.

As discussed in Chapter Two, companion animals from clinics, pounds, and shelters can and are being rendered and used as sources of protein in pet food. Dead-stock removal operations play a major role in the pet food industry. Dead animals, roadkill that cannot be buried at roadside, and in some cases, zoo animals, are picked up by these dead-stock operations. When an animal dies in the field or is killed due to illness or disability, the dead-stock operators pick them up and truck them to the receiving plant. There the dead animal is salvaged for meat or, depending on the state of decomposition, delivered to a rendering plant. At the receiving plants, the animals of value are skinned and viscera removed. Hides of cattle and calves are sold for tanning. The usable meat is removed from the carcass, and covered in charcoal to prevent it from being used for human consumption. Then the meat is frozen, and sold as animal food, which includes pet food.

The packages of this frozen meat must be clearly marked as "unfit for human consumption." The rest of the carcass and poorer quality products including viscera, fat, etcetera, are sent to the rendering facilities. Rendering plants are melting pots for all types of refuse. Restaurant grease and garbage; meats and baked goods long past the expiration dates from supermarkets (Styrofoam trays and shrink-wrap included); the entrails from dead-stock removal operations, and the condemned and contaminated material from slaughterhouses. All of these are rendered.

The slaughterhouses where cattle, pigs, goats, calves, sheep, poultry, and rabbits meet their fate, provide more fuel for rendering. After slaughter, heads, feet, skin, toenails, hair, feathers, carpal and tarsal joints, and mammary glands are removed. This material is sent to rendering. Animals that have died on their way to slaughter are rendered. Cancerous tissue or tumors and worm-infested organs are rendered. Injection sites, blood clots, bone splinters, or extraneous matter are rendered. Contaminated blood is rendered. Stomach and bowels are rendered. Contaminated material containing or having been treated with a substance not permitted by, or in any amount in excess of limits prescribed under the Food and Drug Act or the Environmental Protection Act. In other words, if a carcass contains high levels of drugs or pesticides this material is rendered.

Before rendering, this material from the slaughterhouse is "denatured," which means that the material from the slaughterhouse is covered with a particular substance to prevent it from getting back into the human food chain. In the United States the substances used for denaturing include: crude carbolic acid, fuel oil, or citronella. In Canada the denaturing agent is Birkolene B. When I asked about it, the Ministry of Agriculture would not divulge the composition of Birkolene B, stating its ingredients are a trade secret.[1]

At the rendering plant, slaughterhouse material, restaurant and supermarket refuse, dead-stock, roadkill, and euthanized companion animals are dumped into huge containers. A machine slowly grinds the entire mess. After it is chipped or shredded, it is cooked at temperatures of between 220 degrees F. and 270 degrees F. (104.4 degrees C. to 132.2 degrees C.) for twenty minutes to one hour. The grease or tallow rises to the top, where it is removed from the mixture. This is the source of animal fat in most pet food. The remaining material, the raw, is then put into a press where the moisture is squeezed out. We now have meat and bone meal.

The Association of American Feed Control Officials in its "Ingredient Definitions," describe meat meal as the rendered product from mammal tissue exclusive of blood, hair, hoof, hide, trimmings, manure, stomach, and rumen (the first stomach or the cud of a cud-chewing animal) contents except in such amounts as may occur unavoidably in good processing practices. In an article written by David C. Cooke, "Animal Disposal: Fact and Fiction," Cooke notes, "Can you imagine trying to remove the hair and stomach contents from 600,000 tons of dog and cats prior to cooking them?" It would seem that either the Association of American Feed Control Officials definition of meat meal or meat and bone meal should be redefined or it needs to include a better description of "good factory practices."[2]

When 4-D animals are picked up and sent to these rendering facilities, you can be assured that the stomach contents are not removed. The blood is not drained nor are the horns and hooves removed. The only portion of the animal that might be removed is the hide and any meat that may be salvageable and not too diseased to be sold as raw pet food or livestock feed. The Minister of Agriculture in Quebec made it clear that companion animals are rendered completely.

Petfood Industry magazine states that a pet food manufacturer might reject rendered material for various reasons, including the presence of foreign material (metals, hair, plastic, rubber, glass), off odor, excessive feathers, hair or hog bristles, bone chunks, mold, chemical analysis out of specification, added blood, leather, or calcium carbonate, heavy metals, pesticide contamination, improper grind or bulk density, and insect infestation.[3] Please note that this article states that the manufacturer *might* reject this material, *not* that it does reject this material.

If the label on the pet food you purchase states that the product contains meat meal, or meat and bone meal, it is possible that it is comprised of all the materials listed above.

♦ *Meat*, as defined by the Association of American Feed Control Officials (AAFCO), is the clean flesh derived from slaughtered mammals and is limited to that part of the striate muscle that is skeletal or that which is found in the tongue, diaphragm, heart, or esophagus; with or without the accompanying and overlying fat and the portions of the skin, sinew, nerve, and blood vessels that normally accompany the flesh. When you read on a pet food label that the product contains "real meat," you are getting blood vessels, sinew and so on—hardly the tasty meat that the industry would have us believe it is putting in the food.

♦ *Meat by-products* are the nonrendered, clean parts other than meat derived from slaughtered mammals. It includes, but is not limited to, lungs, spleen, kidneys, brain, livers, blood, bone, partially defatted low temperature fatty tissue, and stomachs and intestines freed of their contents. Again, be assured that if it could be used for human consumption, such as kidneys and livers, it would not be going into pet food. If a liver is found to be infested with worms (liver flukes), if lungs are filled with pneumonia, these can become pet food. However, in Canada, disease-free intestines can still be used for sausage casing for humans instead of pet food.[4]

What about other sources of protein that can be used in pet food?

♦ *Poultry by-product meal* consists of ground, rendered, clean parts of the carcasses of slaughtered poultry, such as necks, feet, undeveloped eggs, and intestines, exclusive of feathers, except in such amounts as might occur unavoidably in good processing practice.

♦ *Poultry-hatchery by-products* are a mixture of egg shells, infertile and unhatched eggs and culled chicks that have been cooked, dried and ground, with or without removal of part of the fat.

♦ *Poultry by-products* include nonrendered clean parts of carcasses of slaughtered poultry such as heads, feet, and viscera, free of fecal content and foreign matter except in such trace amounts as might occur unavoidably in good factory practice. These are all definitions as listed in the AAFCO "Ingredient Definitions."

♦ *Hydrolyzed poultry feather* is another source of protein—not digestible protein, but protein nonetheless. This product results from the treatment under pressure of clean, intact feathers from slaughtered poultry free of additives, and/or accelerators.[5]

We have covered the meat and poultry that can be used in commercial pet foods but according to the AAFCO there are a number of other sources that can make up the protein in these foods. As we venture down the road of these other sources, please be advised to proceed at your own risk if you have a weak stomach.

♦ *Hydrolysed hair* is a product prepared from clean hair treated by heat and pressure to produce a product suitable for animal feeding.

♦ *Spray-dried animal blood* is produced from clean, fresh animal blood, exclusive of all extraneous material such as hair, stomach belching (contents of stomach), and urine, except in such traces as might occur unavoidably in good factory practices.

♦ *Dehydrated food-waste* is any and all animal and vegetable produce picked up from basic food processing sources or institutions where food is processed. The produce shall be picked up daily or sufficiently often so that no decomposition is evident. With this ingredient, it seems that what you don't see won't hurt you.

♦ *Dehydrated garbage* is composed of artificially dried animal and vegetable waste collected sufficiently often that harmful decomposition has not set in and from which have been separated crockery, glass, metal, string, and similar materials.

♦ *Dehydrated paunch products* are composed of the contents of the rumen of slaughtered cattle, dehydrated at temperatures over 212 degrees F. (100 degrees C.) to a moisture content of 12 percent or less, such dehydration is designed to destroy any pathogenic bacteria.

♦ *Dried poultry waste* is a processed animal waste product composed primarily of processed ruminant excreta that has been artificially dehydrated to a moisture content not in excess of 15 percent. It shall contain not less than 12 percent crude protein, not more than 40 percent crude fiber, including straw, wood shavings and so on, and not more than 30 percent ash.

♦ *Dried swine waste* is a processed animal-waste product composed primarily of swine excreta that has been artificially dehydrated to a moisture content not in excess of 15 percent. It shall contain not less than 20 percent crude protein, not more than 35 percent crude fiber, including other material such as straw, woodshavings, or acceptable bedding materials, and not more than 20 percent ash.

♦ *Undried processed animal waste product* is composed of excreta, with or without the litter, from poultry, ruminants, or any other animal except humans, which may or may not include other feed ingredients, and which contains in excess of 15 percent feed ingredients, and which contains in excess of 15 percent moisture. It shall contain no more than 30 percent combined wood, woodshavings, litter, dirt, sand, rocks, and similar extraneous materials.

After reading this list of ingredients for the first time and not really believing that such ingredients could be used in pet food, I sent a fax to the chair of the AAFCO to inquire. "Would the 'Feed Ingredient Definitions' apply to pet food as well as livestock feed?" The reply was as follows, "The feed ingredient definitions approved by the AAFCO apply to all animal feeds, including pet foods, unless specific animal species restrictions are noted."[6]

If a pet food lists "meat by-products" on the label, remember that this is the material that usually comes from the slaughterhouse industry or dead-stock removal operations, classified as condemned or contaminated, unfit for human consumption. Meat meal, meat and bone meal, digests, and tankage (specifically animal tissue including bones and exclusive of hair, hoofs, horns, and contents of digestive tract) are composed of rendered material. The label need not state what the composition of this material is, as each batch rendered would consist of a different material. These are the sources of protein that we are feeding our companion animals.

In 1996 I decided to find out the cost of this "quality" material that the pet food companies purchase from the rendering facilities. Aware that a phone call from an ordinary citizen would not elicit the information I required, I set about forming my own independent pet food company. Stating that my company was about to begin producing quality pet food, I asked for a price quote on meat by-products and meat meal from a Canadian rendering company and from a U.S. rendering company. Both facilities I contacted were more than pleased to provide this information. As I was just a small company and did not require that much material to begin production, the cost was higher than it would have been for one of the large multinationals. Meat and bone meal, with a content of a minimum of 50 percent protein, 12 percent fat, 8 percent moisture, 8 percent calcium, 4 percent phosphorus, and 30 percent ash, could be purchased by me, a small independent company for less than 12¢ (Canadian) a pound.[7] As for the meat by-products the prices varied: liver sold at 21¢ per pound, veal at 22¢ per pound, and lungs for only 12¢ per pound.[8]

The main ingredient in dry food for dogs and cats is corn. However, on further investigation, I found that according to the AAFCO, the list is lengthy as to the corn products that can be used in pet food. These include, but are not limited to the following ingredients.

♦ *Corn flour* is the fine-size hard flinty portions of ground corn containing little or none of the bran or germ.

♦ *Corn bran* is the outer coating of the corn kernel, with little or none of the starchy part of the germ.

♦ *Corn gluten meal* is the dried residue from corn after the removal of the larger part of the starch and germ, and the separation of the bran by the process employed in the wet milling manufacture of corn starch or syrup, or by enzymatic treatment of the endosperm.

Wheat is a constituent found in many pet foods. Again the AAFCO gives descriptive terms for wheat products:

♦ *Wheat flour* consists principally of wheat flour together with fine particles of wheat bran, wheat germ, and the offal from the "tail of the mill." Tail of the mill is nothing more then the sweepings of leftovers after everything has been processed from the week.

♦ *Wheat germ meal* consists chiefly of wheat germ together with some bran and middlings or shorts.

♦ *Wheat middlings* and shorts are also categorized as the fine particles of wheat germ, bran, flour and offal from the "tail of the mill."

Both corn and wheat are usually the first ingredients listed on both dry dog and cat food labels. If they are not the first ingredients, they are the second and third that together make up most of the sources of protein in that particular product. Perhaps the pet food industry is not aware that cats are carnivores and therefore should derive their protein from meat, not grains?

In 1995 one large pet food company, located in California, recalled $20 million worth of its dog food. This food was found to contain vomitoxin. Vomitoxin is formed when grains become wet and moldy. This toxin was found in "wheat screenings" used in the pet food. The FDA did investigate but not out of concern for the more than 250 dogs that became ill after ingesting this food. It investigated because of concerns for human health. The contaminated wheat screenings were the end product of wheat flour that would be used in the making of pasta. Wheat for baking flour requires a higher quality of wheat. Wheat screenings, which are not used for human consumption, can include broken grains, crop and weed seeds, hulls, chaff, joints, straw, elevator or mill dust, sand, and dirt.[9]

♦ *Fat* is usually the second ingredient listed on the pet food labels. Fats can be sprayed directly on the food or mixed with the other ingredients. Fats give off a pungent odor that entices your pet to eat the garbage. These fats are sourced from restaurant grease. This oil is rancid and unfit for human consumption. One of the main sources of fat comes from the rendering plant. This is obtained from the tissues of mammals and/or poultry in the commercial process of rendering or extracting.

An article in *Petfood Industry* magazine does not indicate concern about the impurities in this rendered material as it relates to pet food. Dr. Tim Phillips writes, "Impurities could be small particles of fiber, hair, hide, bone, soil or polyethylene. Or they could be dirt or metal particles picked up after processing (during storage and/or transport). Impurities can cause clogging problems in fat handling screens, nozzles, etc. and contribute to the build-up of sludge in storage tanks."[10]

Other tasty ingredients that can be added to commercial pet food include:

♦ *Beet pulp* is the dried residue from sugar beet, added for fiber, but primarily sugar.

♦ *Soybean meal* is the product obtained by grinding the flakes that remain after the removal of most of the oil from soybeans by a solvent extraction process.

♦ *Powdered cellulose* is purified, mechanically disintegrated cellulose prepared by processing alpha cellulose obtained as a pulp from fibrous plant material. In other words, sawdust.

♦ *Sugar foods by-products* result from the grinding and mixing of inedible portions derived from the preparation and packaging of sugar-based food products such as candy, dry packaged drinks, dried gelatin mixes, and similar food products that are largely composed of sugar.

♦ *Ground almond and peanut shells* are used as another source of fiber.

♦ *Fish* is a source of protein. If you own a cat, just open a can of food that contains fish and watch kitty come running. The parts used are fish heads, tails, fins, bones, and viscera. R.L. Wysong, DVM, states that because the entire fish is not used it does not contain many of the fat soluble vitamins, minerals, and omega-3 fatty acids. If, however, the entire fish is used for pet food, oftentimes it is because the fish contains a high level of mercury or other toxin making it unfit for human consumption. Even fish that was canned for human consumption and that has sat on the shelf past the expiration date will be included. Tuna is used in many cat foods because of its strong odor, which cats find irresistible.

In her book *The New Natural Cat*, Anitra Frazier describes the "tuna junkie" as an expression used by veterinarians to describe a cat hooked on tuna. According to Frazier, "The vegetable oil which it is packed in robs the cat's body of vitamin E which can result in a condition called steatitis."[11] Symptoms of steatitis include extreme nervousness and severe pain when touched. The lack of vitamin E in the diet causes the nerve endings to become sensitive, and can also induce anemia and heart disease. However, excess levels of vitamin E can be toxic. A veterinarian with an understanding of nutrition should be consulted.

One commercial food that most cats and dogs seem to love are the semi-moist foods. These kibble and burger-shaped concoctions are made to resemble real hamburger. However, according to Wendell O. Belfield and Martin Zucker in their book, *How to Have a Healthier Dog*, these are one of the most dangerous of all commercial pet foods.[12] They are high in sugar, laced with dyes, additives, and preservatives, and have a shelf life that spans eternity. One pet owner wrote to me explaining that she had fed her cat some of these semi-moist tidbits. The cat became ill shortly after eating them, and even professional carpet cleaners could not remove the red dye from the carpet where her cat had been ill. In his book, *Pet Allergies: Remedies for an Epidemic*, Alfred Plechner, DVM., writes, "In my opinion, semi-moist foods should be placed in a time capsule to serve as a record of modern technology gone mad."[13]

The pet food industry corrals this material, then mixes, cooks, dries and extrudes the stuff. (Extruding simply means it is pushed through a mold to form the different shapes and to make us think that these so called "chunks" are actually pieces of meat.) Dyes, additives, preservatives are routinely added and they can accumulate in the pet's body.

According to the Animal Protection Institute of America newsletter, "Investigative Report on Pet Food," "Ethoxyquin (an antioxidant preservative), was found in dogs' livers and tissue months after it had been removed from their diet."[14]

After processing, the food is practically devoid of any nutritional value. To make up for what is lacking, vitamins, minerals, amino acids, and supplements are dumped into the mix. If the minerals added are unchelated (chelated means minerals will more readily combine with proteins for better absorption), they will pass through the body virtually unused. Most are added as a premix, and if there is a mistake made in the premix, it can throw off the entire balance. Veterinarians Marty Goldstein and Robert Goldstein have stated that the wrong calcium/magnesium ratio can cause neuromuscular problems.[15] As an example, when I had the commercial pet food tested by Mann Laboratories for my court case, most of the minerals showed excess levels.

The following table shows the Recommended Daily Allowance (RDA) for pets, along with the lab results from the food I had tested:

Minerals	RDA[16]	Lab Results for Popular Dog Food[17]
CALCIUM	11,000	26,100
PHOSPHORUS	9,000	16,500
POTASSIUM	6,000	9,490
MAGNESIUM	400	2,640
IRON	54	295
MANGANESE	4.5	62.1
SELENIUM	0.1	1.2

(These amounts are measured in milligrams per kilogram of food.)

The level of *sodium* found in this food was 6,190 mg. per kg., nearly three teaspoons per kg. of food. When I questioned our veterinarian as to why such high levels were necessary, he informed me that the only reason was to make the food more palatable. Sodium levels are sometimes twenty times greater than the amount needed by a dog.

The pendulum swings widely when it comes to the addition of vitamin and mineral supplements that are added to the diet of your pet. All dogs and cats are not alike and that the addition of supplements will not provide for all that is lacking in the over-processed, low-quality foods.

The prime minerals that are added to pet food include: zinc, iron, and copper. They can, in some cases, cause serious health problems for pets. Zinc, in the form of zinc oxide or proteinate, is added to maintain healthy coat and skin. The Siberian Husky (the breed of dog the pet food company used in the feed test for my court case) is naturally deficient in zinc. The Husky would not be obtaining a sufficient quantity of zinc if he ingested a commercial food, but another dog breed may do fine. Zinc levels over 1,000 ppm can be toxic. The RDA for dogs is approximately 50 mg. per day.

♦ *Iron proteinate, ferrous carbonate, and ferrous sulfate* are necessary for the production of hemoglobin. Deficiencies will manifest themselves as anemia and fatigue. Ferrous sulfate can deplete the vitamin E which many "natural" pet foods use as preservatives.[18]

♦ *Copper oxide, copper proteinate, and copper sulfate* are necessary for converting the iron into hemoglobin. Bedlington Terriers can inherit a condition characterized by an abnormal accumulation of copper in the liver. The liver stores the excess copper that the body is unable to use and when the liver can handle no more, liver disease becomes evident.[19] Copper sulfate, which is found in many pet foods, may pose a major concern to the health of your pet. It has been described as "highly corrosive to plain steel, iron and galvanized pipes."[20] People handling this material have been advised to wear boots, protective gloves and goggles, yet this material may be added to both livestock and pet food. Copper sulfate is stored in the liver, brain, heart, kidneys, and muscles of livestock. It is stable in heat, cold, and light although there is slight decomposition at temperatures about 392 degrees F. (200 degrees C.)

It should be noted too that most of these vitamin and mineral premixes also contain preservatives. This means that your pet is ingesting preservatives from a number of different sources. Artificial flavors, garlic, cheese, and bacon are often added to the foods—to make the food more palatable. These flavors, plus the added dyes, which turn the gray matter a bright red, are to give the consumer the impression that the can of dog or cat food is wholesome.

Next on the list are the preservatives, *BHA* and *BHT*. These two preservatives have long been suspected as being carcinogenic.[21] Both are chemical antioxidants that prevent the fatty contents of the pet food from becoming rancid. With these preservatives, the foods have an endless shelf life. Ethoxyquin, an antioxidant preservative, will be discussed in more detail in Chapter Six, but a few details on this preservative might be appropriate here.

The Farm Chemical Handbook lists Ethoxyquin as a pesticide. *Hawley's Condensed Chemical Dictionary*, Eleventh Edition, lists Ethoxyquin as, "Hazard: Toxic by ingestion." *The Consumers Dictionary of Food Additives* lists Ethoxyquin as a "yellow liquid antioxidant and herbicide. It has been found to cause liver tumors in newborn mice." Ethoxyquin in sold by PennWalt under the name of Deccoquin and has a very prominent skull and crossbones on the label that reads "Caution/-Poison" in large print.[22]

Pet food companies need not state on the label that Ethoxyquin has been added to the food unless the pet food company itself added the substance. If it is added to the fat at the rendering facility, or added to the grain at the feed mill, or added to any pet food ingredient before it arrives at the pet food company, the label does not need to list Ethoxyquin

Many of the grains used in commercial pet food contain levels of herbicides, pesticides, and fungicides that are cancer-causing agents. Little, if any, testing or research is undertaken in this area as data are limited.

* * *

"Complete and Balanced" or "100 Percent Nutritionally Complete"—what do these statements really mean? The pet food industry can usually make these claims based on feed trials. A feeding trial is when the food is fed to dogs over a period ranging from ten to twenty-six weeks. In many cases, these dogs are in cages, under artificial lights, and walk only on concrete.[23]

Some of these foods that were "feed tested" and found to be "Complete and Balanced" or "100 Percent Nutritionally Complete" caused many serious health problems in pets. Some of these problems include dilated cardiomyopathy in dogs and cats, potassium depletion in cats, and retinal atrophy in cats. Retinal atrophy is caused by the lack of taurine, an amino acid found primarily in meat. Because of the quality of the ingredients and the overprocessing of these foods, it was found that they lacked this important nutrient. This disease can lead to blindness in cats.[24]

In 1993 excess levels of iodine were found in cat foods. A survey showed that one in every three hundred cats in New York was battling a thyroid tumor. This equals 200,000 cases a year out of a cat population of sixty-two million in the United States.[25]

Bob Parkey of the Kansas City-based Iomate Corporation, "believes that fluctuation of the iodine levels, due to the inability of crystalline iodine to mix properly and stay stable in the typical pet food formulation, is the major contributing factor to iodine-associated problems such as hyperthyroidism (over-active thyroid) in the cat and hypothyroidism (deficient-thyroid function) in the dog."[26]

The Veterinary Record reports vitamin K deficiency in cats fed diets high in salmon and tuna. Queens and kittens have died and on autopsy, hepatic and/or gastrointestinal hemorrhages have been found.[27]

Petfood Industry magazine discussed another deficiency, which it refers to as the "Vexing Feline Problem."

> **Petfood manufacturers should take special notice of the osteoclastic resorptive lesions or cervical neck lesions being seen in cats. Preliminary studies have shown that they are not related to the metabolic acid pH created by modern diets. However, the lesions have only been noticed in the last twenty years, when there has been a huge shift to commercial foods.[28]**

Daily, veterinarians treat cats for feline urological syndrome (FUS). If left untreated FUS can kill a cat in a very short time. This disease has been blamed on high ash, high phosphorus, and according to some veterinarians, high magnesium levels in commercial pet food.

These foods have been touted as complete and balanced when in actuality they were causing untold health problems and death in our pets. Dr. Wysong has aptly described the "complete and balanced" diet: "Each time regulatory agencies convene to decide how much of which nutrients comprise 100 percent completeness, debate always ensues and standards usually change. This not only proves that what they claimed before was not '100 Percent Nutritionally Complete,' but this should also make us highly suspicious about what they now claim to be 100 percent complete." [29]

Looking to nature may provide us with a more accurate definition of what "100 percent nutritionally complete" should be. In studies done on the eating habits of dingoes in Western Australia, it is noted that rabbits were a large part of the diet of these dogs. Feral cats in Victoria ingested rabbits and a small percentage of grass and twigs. Vegetable matter was of low levels and no mention was made of soy, wheat, rice, etcetera. Animals in the wild do not ingest grains as such, but the prime ingredients in most commercial dry food are corn, wheat, soy, and rice. Grains are even cheaper than the meat meals and by-products and are used in both dry cat and dog food.

Because some pet food is purported to be "100 percent complete and balanced," consumers believe that their pets are obtaining everything they require from these commercial diets. This assertion must be challenged. Feeding trials use various breeds of dogs, but the choice is usually Beagles. No feeding trial encompasses all breeds, from Chihuahuas to Saint Bernards. Feeding trials are conducted over a period of weeks and it is hoped that your dog or cat might survive a little longer than that. Dr. Wysong writes, "In order for nutritionists and manufacturers to produce "100 percent complete and balanced" pet food they must first know 100 percent about nutrition."[30] No scientist would state that everything is known about nutrition, human or animal; hence, "100 percent complete and balanced" is an invalid claim.

Many pet owners have a fear of feeding their pets even a raw carrot as it might tip the so-called balanced processed commercial foods. "Would you accept the advice of a pediatrician who told you that you should feed your child only what is in a bag or can every day, every meal, for the child's entire life and never supplement anything to it?" queries Dr. Wysong in a 1995 brochure, "Pet Health Alert." "No raw carrots, no apples, no freshly cooked cereal? I hope not! Then why accept such advice regarding your pet?"

A typical scenario is this: You have fed your dog or cat a particular brand of food for six months and your pet is doing well. A new can, a new bag of the same product and suddenly your pet develops diarrhea, vomiting, or gas. You assume that your pet has picked up a virus or someone has fed your pet human food. You reason that this is the same pet food that you have fed for six months without a problem, therefore it could not be the food. Wrong! Perhaps the meat meal, tankage, or digest has changed (which it usually does from batch to batch). Perhaps a different grain has been used in the food (if it is cheaper it will be used). Perhaps a new preservative has been added. Labels do not have to state any changes in their ingredients for six months.[31]

Veterinarians see pets every day who suffer the effects of commercial diets. As one veterinarian put it, "All I can do is treat the symptoms." In 1996 the pet food industry was producing nearly eight million tons of pet food each year. According to Jim Corbin, DVM, of the pet food industry, this is feeding fifty-three million dogs and fifty-six million cats in the United States "with a value estimated conservatively at $9 billion, plus exports estimated to be an additional $550 million."[32]

Reading Dog and Cat Food Labels

How many people buying pet food actually read the label? How many understand what the ingredients actually are in these brands of pet food? I have included a list of ingredients from a few labels from both canned and dry, dog and cat food. Perhaps this may shed some light on the ingredients in these foods. There are no whole grains, no fresh meats, no pure oils. Most of the ingredient lists are composed of vitamins, minerals, and supplements added to compensate for the inferior ingredients. Also remember that when the industry adds ingredients in small amounts, they need not list them on the label. The following ingredients are listed in the order that most of them appear on many pet food labels

Dry Dog Food

GROUND CORN: ground or chopped corn. According to the AAFCO, must not contain more than 4 percent foreign matter.

POULTRY BY-PRODUCT MEAL: ground, rendered parts of the carcasses of poultry. Necks, feet, undeveloped eggs, intestines and birds that are condemned for human consumption.

RICE FLOUR: finely powdered material, usually the end process of milling. Very low nutrition value.

MEAT MEAL: rendered product from animal tissue (need not state what animal). Any mammal can be used.

BEET SUGAR: the dried residue from the sugar beet..

POULTRY FAT: (preserved with BHA): obtained from the tissue of rendered poultry. Contains no added free fatty acids.

DRIED WHOLE EGGS: this can be broken eggs, rejects from hatchery operations or eggs unfit for human consumption.

FISH MEAL: dried ground tissue of fish. As this is not the entire fish, it does not contain many of the fat-soluble vitamins, omega-3 fatty acids or minerals.

POULTRY DIGEST: material that results from chemical or enzymatic hydrolysis of poultry tissue.

BREWER'S DRIED YEAST: dried residue from the brewing industry. Cooked yeast fractions that the brewers cannot use.

MONOSODIUM PHOSPHATE: emulsifying agent.

CHOLINE CHLORIDE: member of the B complex.

DI-METHIONINE: an amino acid.

POTASSIUM CHLORIDE: mineral. Potassium salt of hydrochloric acid.

ASCORBIC ACID: vitamin C.

VITAMIN E SUPPLEMENT

COPPER SULFATE: mineral. Copper salt of sulfuric acid.

ETHOXYQUIN: a preservative.

ZINC OXIDE: mineral.

MANGANESE SULFATE: manganese salt of sulfuric acid.

MANGANESE OXIDE: mineral. Oxide form of manganese.

BIOTIN SUPPLEMENT: vitamin K.

VITAMIN A ACETATE: water-dispersible source of vitamin A.

CALCIUM PANTHENATE: vitamin B5.

VITAMIN B12

NIACIN: vitamin B6.

THIAMIN MONONITRATE: vitamin B1.

COPPER OXIDE: mineral.

MENADIONE DIMETHYLPRIMIDINOL BISULFITE: source of Vitamin K.

RIBOFLAVIN SUPPLEMENT: vitamin B2.

INOSITOL: supplement.

PYRIDOXINE HYDROCHLORIDE: vitamin B6.

VITAMIN D3: from animal origin.

POTASSIUM IODIDE: potassium salt of iodic acid (iodine).

FOLIC ACID: vitamin B9.

SODIUM SELENITE: mineral. Sodium salt of sulfuric acid.

Canned Dog Food

MEAT BY-PRODUCTS: nonrendered material. Meat derived from slaughterhouse mammals. Can contain condemned and contaminated meat. Includes, but is not limited to, lungs, kidneys, brains, liver, blood, and bone.

CHICKEN: animals deemed unfit for human consumption. These may be chickens that have died from disease or have been found to contain excess levels of drugs or hormones.

WATER

BEEF: meat unfit for human consumption. This may consist of diseased material or meat containing high levels of drugs, heavy metals, or pesticides.

BREWER'S RICE: rice sections that have been discarded from the human food manufacturing of wort or beer, which contain pulverized, dried, spent hops. Little, if any, nutritional value.

SOY FLOUR: Dr. Wysong describes this ingredient as "powdered material from screened and graded product after removal, by a mechanical or solvent extraction process, of most of the oil from selected and dehulled soybeans." Removing this oil reduces the essential fatty acids, antioxidants, and vitamin content.

POTASSIUM CHLORIDE: mineral. Potassium salt of hydrochloric acid.

FERROUS SULFATE: 20 percent elemental iron.

ZINC OXIDE: mineral.

MANGANOUS OXIDE: mineral.

COPPER SULFATE: mineral. Copper salt of sulfuric acid.

CALCIUM IODATE: mineral. Calcium salt of iodic acid (iodine)

SODIUM SELENITE: mineral. Sodium salt of selenious acid.

CHOLINE CHLORIDE: member of the B complex.

VITAMINS E, D-3, AND B12: vitamin D-3 is a normal, active form of vitamin D in animals.

VITAMIN A ACETATE: water-dispersible source of vitamin A.

D-CALCIUM PANTOTHENATE: vitamin B5.

THIAMIN MONONITRATE: vitamin B1.

PYRIDOXINE HYDROCHLORIDE: vitamin B6.

RIBOFLAVIN: vitamin B2.

FOLIC ACID: vitamin B9.

Canned Dog Food

WATER

LIVER: source of the liver is not stated. Unfit for human consumption, liver used in pet food can be diseased and riddled with liver flukes.

MEAT BY-PRODUCTS: nonrendered material. Meat derived from slaughtered mammals. Can contain condemned and contaminated material from slaughterhouse facilities. Can include, but is not limited to, lungs, brain, spleen, kidneys, liver, blood, and bone.

WHEAT SHORTS: offal from the milling process of wheat.

RICE: nonspecific as to the form of this rice, i.e., rice flour, rice bran, rice hulls, chipped and broken rice or rice polishings.

CELLULOSE: a pulp from fibrous plant. Also has been described as sawdust.

DICALCIUM PHOSPHATE: mineral.

CALCIUM CARBONATE: mineral.

IODIZED SALT

POTASSIUM CHLORIDE: mineral. Potassium salt of hydrochloric acid.

BREWER'S DRIED YEAST: dried reside from the brewing industry. Cooked yeast fractions that the brewers cannot use.

VITAMIN E ACETATE: water-dispersible source of Vitamin E.

VEGETABLE OIL: nonspecific as to the type of oil.

CHOLINE CHLORIDE: member of the B complex vitamins.

THIAMINE MONONITRATE: vitamin B1.

RIBOFLAVIN SUPPLEMENT: vitamin B2.

VITAMIN A ACETATE: water-dispersible source of Vitamin A.

BIOTIN: Vitamin H.

VITAMIN D3: D-activated animal sterol.

VITAMIN B12: Supplement.

Canned Cat Food

MEAT BY-PRODUCTS: nonrendered material. Meat derived from slaughtered mammals. Can contain condemned and contaminated material from slaughterhouses. Meat by-products include, but are not limited to, lungs, spleen, brains, liver, kidneys, blood, and bones.

BEEF: Material from cattle, again unfit for human consumption. Limited to that part of the striate muscle that is skeletal or which is found in the tongue, in the diaphragm, in the heart or esophagus. Can contain sinew, nerve, and blood vessels.

WATER

FISH: Head, fins, tail, skin, bones, and viscera. As this is not the whole fish it does not contain many of the fat-soluble vitamins, minerals, or omega-3 fatty acids.

BREWER'S RICE: Dr. Wysong describes this ingredient, "Polished rice sections which have been discarded from the human manufacturing of wort or beer and which may contain pulverized dried, spent hops." Nutritional value of this ingredient is almost nil.

TRICALCIUM PHOSPHATE: mineral. Calcium salt of phosphoric acid.

GUAR GUM: mucilage (glue). Used as a stabilizer.

POTASSIUM CHLORIDE: mineral. Potassium salt of hydrochloric acid.

CARAMEL COLOR: no nutritional value.

IRON OXIDE: mineral. Commonly known as "rust."

SALT

TAURINE: amino acid.

CARRAGEENIN: seaweed.

CHOLINE CHLORIDE: member of the vitamin B complex.

ZINC SULFATE: mineral.

VITAMINS E, A, B12, D3: vitamin D3 is described "by activation of a sterol fraction of animal origin."

FERROUS SULFATE: 20 percent elemental iron.

THIAMINE MONONITRATE: Vitamin B1.

MANGANESE SULFATE: mineral. Manganese salt of sulfuric acid.

NIACIN PYRIDOXINE HYDROCHLORIDE: vitamin B6.

NATURAL FLAVOR: no nutritional value.

CALCIUM PANTOTHENATE: vitamin B5.

RIBOFLAVIN SUPPLEMENT: vitamin B2.

MENADIONE SODIUM BISULFITE COMPLEX: vitamin K.

FOLIC ACID: vitamin B9.

POTASSIUM IODIDE: mineral. Potassium and iodine.

BIOTIN: vitamin K.

SODIUM SELENITE: mineral. Sodium salt of selenious acid.

Dry Cat Food

POULTRY BY-PRODUCT MEAL: rendered poultry, neck, feet, undeveloped eggs, and intestines. This may also include feather and animals that have died from unknown causes.

GROUND YELLOW CORN: ground or chopped yellow corn. Yellow corn is one of the lowest nutritional varieties of corn.

CORN GLUTEN MEAL: dried residue from corn after the removal of starch, germ, and bran. Little, if any, nutritional value.

BREWER'S RICE: polished rice sections that have been discarded from the human manufacturing of wort or beer and which may contain pulverized, dried, spent hops. Little nutritional value.

ANIMAL FAT PRESERVED WITH BHA: from tissue of animals or poultry extracted in the rendering process. Devoid of free fatty acids.

FISH MEAL: dried ground tissue of fish. As this is not the entire fish it does not contain many of the fat-soluble vitamins, omega-3 fatty acids, or minerals.

WHEAT FLOUR: together with particles of wheat and bran and the left-over of the milling of wheat.

GROUND WHEAT: as above only a courser grind.

SPRAY DRIED WHEY: dried by spraying on the surface of a heated drum. High in lactose.

POULTRY LIVER (ENZYMATIC) HYDROLYSATE: liver of poultry, unfit for human consumption. It is subjected to acid hydrolysis.

BREWER'S DRIED YEAST: left over from the beer brewing industry.

BEET PULP: dried residue from sugar beets. Pure sugar.

SODIUM ACID PYROPHOSPHATE: mineral. Salt of pyrophosphate acid.

POTASSIUM CHLORIDE: mineral. Potassium salt of hydrochloric acid.

SALT

CHOLINE CHLORIDE: a member of the vitamin B complex.

TAURINE: an amino acid.

DI-METHIONINE: an amino acid.

FERROUS SULFATE: 20 percent elemental iron.

ZINC OXIDE: mineral.

VITAMIN E: supplement.

YUCCA SCHIDIGERA EXTRACT: supplement.

NIACIN: vitamin B6.

SODIUM SELENITE: mineral. Sodium salt of selenious acid.

COPPER SULFATE: mineral. Copper salt of sulfuric acid.

VITAMIN A: supplement.

CALCIUM PANTOTHENATE: vitamin B5.

MANGANOUS OXIDE: mineral.

THIAMINE MONONITRATE: vitamin B1.

MENADIONE DIMETHYLPYRIMIDINOL BISULFITE: classified as "Commercial Feed Grade Vitamin."

PYRIDOXINE HYDROCHLORIDE: vitamin B6.

D-ACTIVATED ANIMAL STEROL: vitamin D3.

RIBOFLAVIN: vitamin B2.

ETHYLENODIAMINE DIHYDRIODIDE: iodine.

BIOTIN SUPPLEMENT: vitamin H.

VITAMIN B12: supplement.

FOLIC ACID: vitamin B9.

Chapter Five

Hidden Hazards in Pet Food:
Drugs, Heavy Metals, Pesticides, and Pathogens

When it comes to understanding what is included in pet food, labels are extremely vague in showing the actual ingredients used. Labels do not indicate the hidden hazards that lurk in most cans and bags of pet food. Hazards that can have an insidious effect on the health and well-being of our pets. Hormones, pesticides, pathogens, heavy metals, and drugs are just a few of the hidden contaminates.

Sodium pentobarbital, discussed in Chapter Two, is a barbiturate used to euthanize companion animals and, to some extent, livestock. When animals eat pet food that has gone through the rendering process, it is likely that they are ingesting a euthanizing drug. According to Dr. Ashley Robinson, an expert on sodium pentobarbital, "No further studies have been carried out, to my knowledge, on residues from sodium pentobarbital."[1] Consumers have no way of estimating the levels of this drug in pet food, and the label does not tell us. Each batch of rendered material contains a different percentage of animal sources. Testing would have to be done on a can-to-can or bag-to-bag basis to determine if there are any residues from these drugs, and if so, how much.

Voluntary organizations such as the Association of American Feed Control Officials, (AAFCO), Canadian Veterinary Medical Association (CVMA), Pet Food Manufacturers Association (PFMA), and even government agencies do not undertake testing for sodium pentobarbital. Perhaps these organizations feel that such small amounts of these drugs would not have a detrimental effect on the health of our pets.

In addition, some 50 percent of the antibiotics manufactured in the United States are dumped into animal feed, according to *Food Chemical News*, an industry newsletter.[2] On factory farms, pigs, cows, veal calves, and chickens are continually fed antibiotics, primarily penicillin and tetracycline. In a vain attempt to eradicate the many ills that befall these animals—pneumonia, intestinal disease, stress, rhinitis, mastitis, and so forth—drugs are a routine addition to their diets. Factory farming of animals for human consumption has become a major contributor to these many ills. This high-level use of drugs means millions of dollars for the pharmaceutical companies. And for the farmers, a shorter time period before these animals can be slaughtered because the animals quickly fatten up with the use of hormones and drugs. However, humans and pet companions are the ultimate losers because it ends up in the food we consume.

The U.S. Centers for Disease Control, Natural Resources Defense Council, and the U.S. Food and Drug Administration state, "The levels of antibiotics and other contaminants in commercially raised meat constitute a serious threat to the health of the consumer." New and more powerful antibiotics are being developed to treat human illnesses because the wonder drugs of the 1950s and 1960s, such as penicillin, tetracycline, and streptomycin are no longer viable in treating disease because humans have built up a resistance to them.

Millions of farm animals are treated with antibiotics. When these animals die in the field they are considered 4-D animals and are shipped to rendering. If they die on their way to slaughter or are condemned as unfit for human consumption at the time of slaughter, they end up being rendered too. The vicious cycle is continued with rendered animals, laced with a wide array of drugs, being fed to animals that are being given more of the same drug—resulting in a double dose.

Animals are removed from antibiotics, usually thirty days prior to slaughter, so that the drugs will be out of their system at the time of slaughter. However, if excess levels are found or injection sites are observed, the animals, or areas in question, are removed and sent to rendering plants for livestock and pet food.

Rendering temperatures range from 250 degrees F. to 260 degrees F. (121 degrees C. to 126 degrees C.)[3] I've questioned a number of scientists to ascertain if rendering temperatures would degrade these drugs. The only information available relates to the cooking temperatures of meat for human consumption. It has been found that at temperatures of 375 F., ampicillin degrades 60 percent, penicillin degrades 87 percent, tetracycline degrades 70 percent, and chloramphenicol degrades 30 percent. Mark Papich, DVM., Associate Professor of Clinical Pharmacology, North Carolina State University, writes:

> Although some drugs may degrade at cooking temperatures, the drug breakdown products, or degradation products may remain. The degradation products are, for some drugs, still active, or more toxic than the parent drug. Turkeys and chickens are given tetracycline to treat respiratory diseases and E-coli. Cattle and swine are given the drug to treat pneumonia, *E-coli*, and *Salmonella*. For the most part, these drugs are administered as a preventive measure, not actually used to treat an illness.[4]

PENICILLIN, another extensively used antibiotic, is administered to swine, sheep, cattle, and horses to treat pneumonia. The withdrawal time for this drug is seven to ten days.

CHLORAMPHENICOL, a powerful antibiotic but one that was never approved for use in livestock in the United States seems to be the drug of choice by some farmers to treat bacteria infections in livestock. Although not approved for use, this drug can be obtained on the black market or from unscrupulous veterinarians.[5] In the last few years, chloramphenicol has been banned from use in Canada. This drug has been linked to aplastic anemia in humans.[6] (In aplastic anemia the production of red and white blood cells and platelets fall dramatically and causes low resistance to infection and bruising.)

Although banned from use in the treatment of livestock, chloramphenicol is still approved for use in the treatment of some infections in dogs. Remember, dogs can be rendered and fed back to livestock or processed into pet food. Being heat stable—which means it is not easily degraded at high temperatures—this drug withstands the temperatures of rendering, degrading only 30 percent at 375 degrees F. (190.5 degrees C.) Cats have been found to be extremely sensitive to this drug and ingestion of very small amounts can be fatal, according to William Hare, DVM, of the National Animal Poison Control Center.[7]

Of great concern to the pork industry a few years ago, were SULFONAMIDES, specifically SULFAMETHAZINE, an antibiotic added to swine feed. High levels of these drugs remained in animal tissue and many were rejected for slaughter. This family of drugs is heat stable. Pigs rejected for slaughter, dying in the field or dying on their way to slaughter, are most likely to end up in pet food.

Extensive use is being made of growth hormones to fatten up meat-producing animals. Implantation of these hormones has given rise to concerns of residues in the human food chain. These implants are usually put in the animal's ear and the drug is slowly released into the animal's system. Cattle heads, *including* implants, are rendered. In the book, *Animal Nutrition*, the authors state:

> **Extensive use is being made of synthetic and purified estrogens, androgens, progestogens, and growth hormones to stimulate the growth and fattening of meat-producing animals. Some of these have given important increases in the rate and efficiency of gain or in the quality of the food products that result. There is concern, however, about possible harmful effects of any residues of these materials in the meat: Meat, found to contain these drugs, can be used for pet food.[8]**

One hormone that has gained much notoriety in the last few years is *bovine growth hormone* (BGH), also known as *bovine somatotropin* (BST). Marketed by a number of companies including Monsanto, BGH is a hormone that simulates a natural hormone and when it is injected into cows, it increases milk production. Canada, many European communities, Australia, and New Zealand have banned the use of this hormone—so far.[9] Surprisingly, many Canadians might inadvertently purchase dairy products containing BGH because many products, imported from the United States, contain it. (The FDA approved the use of BGH in the United States.) Foods containing BGH need not indicate this on the label.

Monsanto argues that this hormone is safe. But Monsanto also touted the virtues of Agent Orange, a herbicide used during the Vietnam War. (An Illinois court found that Monsanto had altered the results of a study conducted on workers who had been exposed to the deadly dioxins in Agent Orange. It is now known to be a cancer-causing agent.)

We now have antibiotics, sulfonamides, and growth hormones—perhaps minute amounts—but, nonetheless, finding their way into pet food. With no research in this area, as it relates to companion animals, we cannot ascertain the effect on our pets.

In addition to all the other substances already mentioned, we also have to consider PESTICIDES. Most often these are poured or sprayed on cattle to repel flies and insects. In addition, they are sprayed and dusted on crops. Most pesticides withstand the rendering process without undergoing degradation.

INSECTICIDES used on grains, which also can be applied to livestock for pest control, possess residual action that can persist for months. Pesticides and insecticides can be stored in fat, which is rendered, and excreted in milk. Some of the potent insecticides, chlorinated hydrocarbons, although banned from use, are still showing up as residues in livestock tissue. CHLORINATED HYDROCARBONS used in weed and pest control can remain in soil and on grazing crops for years. All of the hydrocarbons are heat stable and were withdrawn due to the grave concern for the health of humans ingesting food or milk from animals and crops that had been sprayed with these potent chemicals. TOXAPHENE, considered to be four to five times more toxic than DDT, is still being used despite the ban.[10]

In 1988, 91 percent of staphylococcal infections were resistant to penicillin. The major contributing cause was the "breeding of antibiotic resistant bacteria due to the routine feeding of antibiotics to livestock in factory farming."[11]

Salmonella, which has been linked to illness and death in thousands of humans over the years, can be a contributing cause of gastrointestinal illness in our pets. *Salmonella* and *E-coli* contamination have become major concerns in dry and canned pet food, in particular the dry food. Within thirty-six hours of ingestion the pet will display the symptoms of vomiting and diarrhea. *Salmonella* can also contaminate any human food that the product comes into contact.[12]

Jeff Bender and Ashley Robinson, both veterinarians at the Department of Clinical and Population Sciences at the University of Minnesota, in their research on *Salmonella* write:

> **An epidemic in a Minnesota cattery several years ago was caused by *Salmonella* newport and *S. typhimrium*. There was severe mortality in kittens over a six-month period which eventually resulted in a decision to depopulate. The most likely source of this infection was the feeding of so called "4-D" meat (meat from dead dying, diseased, and debilitated livestock), as *Salmonellas* were isolated from this particular product.[13]**

Raw meat sold by the dead-stock removal operations is rife with this bacteria. Freezing has only a minimal effect on the destruction of *Salmonella*. Cooking will destroy it, but in the process everything the meat touches is contaminated. The FDA warns, "This meat may present a health hazard to animals that consume it and the people who handle it." This material is also sold to the pet food industry as a source of protein. Cattle, swine, and poultry are infected with *Salmonella*. Half of the chicken and turkey sold in supermarkets contain this bacteria. Information researched by the nonprofit organization, Farm Sanctuary, states: "At least 60 percent of U.S. poultry is contaminated with *Salmonella*, camphylobacter, *E-coli*, or other micro-organisms. Each year 6.5 million people get sick, and at least 1,000 people die from contaminated poultry."[14] This is why we are advised to cook meat thoroughly.

The eradication of *Salmonella* in rendered material has been the goal of the National Renderers Association. This is a formidable task, given the fact that recontamination occurs so easily. Tons of rendered material pass through rendering plants on a daily basis. Rendered material is tested only once a month for this deadly bacteria. Testing for *Salmonella* is not a complicated process. The Vicam Microbiological Testing System provides "in house" testing equipment that it claims is "simple, little training required" and "economical." "The procedure is simple. Magnetic beads, coated with antibodies that bind to *Salmonella* are used to isolate *Salmonella* and *Salmonella enteritidis* from samples. The beads are planted onto agar growth medium. After incubation, suspect colonies are examined by a method giving a visual score."[15] Every rendering facility, every pet food company, should be testing for this bacteria as well as *E-coli* on an a regular basis.

Just as life-threatening are the mycotoxins. Contained in contaminated grain, some of these toxins can be deadly. Caused by cool, damp conditions in the growing and storing of wheat, corn, peanuts, and other grain crops, mycotoxins can cause symptoms ranging from mild stomach upset to death in both humans and pets. According to *Petfood Industry* magazine, "In 1995 the U.S. grain, feed, pet food and food industry experienced the worst year in history for litigation involving mycotoxin related law suits. A low estimate for 1995 mycotoxin litigation costs totals more than $500 million dollars, according to Romer Labs, Union, Missouri."[16]

The family of mycotoxins are numerous and include: aflatoxin B1, ergotism, citrinin, vomitoxin, zearaleone, and ochratoxin, to name a few. In 1996 vomitoxin levels in wheat and corn were very high. A large number of crops, grown for human consumption, were downgraded for use only in animal and pet food.

AFLATOXIN B1 is among one of the most toxic substances known to humankind. Measured in parts per billion (ppb), minute quantities can kill animals and humans. In the case of grains grown for human consumption, testing for this toxin is mandatory. However, this is not the case within the pet food industry. In June 1988, *The Veterinary Journal* reported a number of cases of dogs that had succumbed to aflatoxin B1 in their diets. Aflatoxins have been shown to cause liver cancer in laboratory animals at levels as low as one part per billion. Peanut shells, a source of fiber used in some commercial pet foods, are one of the prime sources of aflatoxins.[17]

FUSARIUM, the mold or fungi that causes vomitoxin, is rampant in both the United States and Canada. The 1996 crops in the Province of Ontario experienced the worst outbreak in the last five or six years. A 1996 article in the *London Free Press* reported, "$150 million in revenue has been lost. By midsummer, virtually all of the harvested crop was of such poor quality it had to be downgraded to low-priced animal feed (this includes pet food), instead of milled into flour."[18] To control the outbreak, it has been suggested that fusarium-contaminated grain be mixed with uncontaminated grain, making it a more viable medium for use in pet food. If the contaminated and uncontaminated grains are not mixed thoroughly, areas of contaminated grains, also known as "hot spots," develop. Depending on the volume processed, batches of pet food could still be contaminated. The safest method to prevent outbreaks is to eliminate entirely any grains or grain by-products contaminated with any toxin. Antibiotics are ineffective in treating vomitoxicoses, so prevention is the best cure.

ZINC, COPPER, and IRON are minerals listed on the labels of most pet food. The lab that tested the dog food in my court case showed other metals contained in this product. Metals that were not and did not need to be listed on the label include silver, beryllium, cadmium, bismuth, cobalt, manganese, barium, molybdenum, nickel, lead, strontium, vanadium, tungsten, phosphorus, titanium, chromium, sodium, potassium, aluminum, calcium, magnesium, and selenium.[19] Some of these are trace elements that are found naturally, but there is still the question of TUNGSTEN, an alloy. The only plausible explanation in the lab report I received is that tungsten comes from the machinery used in the processing of the pet food. Little information is available on the toxic properties of tungsten.

LEAD was also found in the sample of dog food I sent to the lab; 3.27 mg. per kg. of food. Research conducted at the Connecticut Agricultural Experiment Station detected "quantities" of lead in liver and kidney organs. These organ meats are a prime ingredient in many canned pet foods. The results of the testing undertaken in Connecticut indicated that of the canned cat food tested, a cat ingesting six ounces of food per day, the daily intake of lead would range from 0.15 to 1.2 mg. For the dog food tested, a dog ingesting fifteen ounces would be receiving levels of 0.43 to 2.4 mg. per day. Also tested in the Connecticut research were two types of dry cat food. The results stated, "Based on consumption of 120 g. per day, the cat would ingest 0.42 and 0.72 mg. of lead, or 1.4 and 2.4 times the 0.3 level considered unsafe for a child. By comparison, a dog or cat is much smaller than a child."[20]

Dr. Wendell Belfield, working with a California pet foundation, determined that "lead levels in cats suffering from feline leukemia were extremely high. Mercury was also found to be present in abnormally high levels...supplied probably by dietary fish."[21]

The FDA and Health and Welfare Canada would be very concerned if lead levels as high as those shown were found in the human food chain. Because this is not human food but food for dogs and cats, the government agencies are not concerned. No testing is undertaken by state officials for pathogens, heavy metals, pesticides, or drugs in pet food. These are but a tiny fragment of the hundreds of contaminates which we, unintentionally, are feeding our pets on a daily basis.

How often have you taken your pet to the veterinarian and the treatment prescribed is antibiotics? Our pets bodies have become deluged with antibiotics, and therefore they can become resistant to the many drugs used to treat viral and bacterial infections. When one drug proves ineffective, another is prescribed, and then another. When all else fails, many veterinarians will suggest STEROIDS. You can end up with enough half-used drugs for your pet to fill an apothecary.

Photo: Sumner Fowler

Chapter Six

Pet Food Regulations in the United States and Canada

The regulations of the pet food industry in the United States are complex and convoluted. Animal feed, which includes livestock and pet food, fall under the jurisdiction of the Food and Drug Administration, Center for Veterinary Medicine (FDA/CVM). The Association of American Feed Control Officials (AAFCO) sets guidelines with regard to the labeling of pet food. It is up to each state to adopt these guidelines. The National Research Council (NRC) published recommended minimum nutrient concentrations based upon a review of literature and research it conducted. Some of its research is conducted on live animals.

During my investigations, I was provided with some insight into this research. I received a letter from a person (who requested anonymity) and who had taken a course in canine nutrition at Cornell University. This is a university that undertakes research for the NRC. This letter from the Cornell contact indicates just how questionable research is for pet nutrition. The letter stated:

> At Cornell, I viewed slides of some of their studies. I will never forget them. I saw Great Dane puppies that were deprived of all calcium and turned into "jelly dogs," they had no bones. The test conclusion: "dogs have a nutritional need for calcium"—I kid you not, a direct quote from the scientists. Another set of pups was forced into convulsive seizures through lack of

magnesium. Pregnant Beagles were given massive overdoses of A to produce cleft palates in their short-lived pups. Most of the studies involve massive deficiencies or overdoses—not what a dog (or person) might consume in a natural species-specific diet...Unfortunately, I saw many, many other slides of malformed dogs (mostly pups) that were torturously kept alive just long enough to determine what might be put into commercial pet food products. The worst of it is that many of the studies acknowledge the information does not pertain to all dogs, since different breeds have different nutritional requirements. So many of the test results are "'inconclusive" and full of "maybes" and "might needs."[1]

One other group, The Pet Food Institute, is a pet food industry association representing the interests of various pet food companies. Over the years, I have written and faxed this association numerous times in order to ascertain its policies regarding the industry. Not one representative has ever acknowledged any of my correspondence.

When my quest for information on the regulations of the pet food industry in the United States began, I assumed that the U.S. Department of Agriculture, Animal and Plant Health Inspection Service (USDA/APHIS), would be involved. I found that this agency only administers the Animal Welfare Act that deals with minimum standards of humane care and treatment of animals sold into the pet trade, transported commercially, exhibited to the public, and used in research.[2] This agency did not have any input into ingredients or regulations as they pertain to commercial pet food.

Next, I contacted the United States Department of Agriculture, Food Safety and Inspection Service (USDA/FSIS) to see if this agency was involved with regulations of the pet food industry. I found its responsibility relates to meat and poultry for the human food chain only. Its mandate is to insure that meat and poultry are safe, wholesome, and accurately labeled.[3]

Soon after I became aware of the FDA/CVM. My first query to this department was rather vague, but the reply was quick in coming. From there, further replies to my questions eventually led to waiting for months for answers. Perhaps the representatives were fed up with what they stated were my "continued and expanding questions."[4] When all else failed and the FDA/CVM did not respond for a month or two, I sent a fax to Dr. David Kessler who, at the time, was Commissioner of the FDA. This would always elicit a response from the appropriate party. The last paragraph of these letters would inform me that if I had any further questions to address them directly to the FDA/CVM, not to Dr. Kessler.[5]

What are the responsibilities of the FDA/CVM relating to commercial pet food? Its primary duties are to health claims made by the pet food companies, for example those companies that claim their foods "will prevent Feline Urological Syndrome (FUS)." The FDA/CVM will check to see if research supports these companies' claims.

The FDA/CVM's duties also include the labeling of products: proper identification of the product, net quantity statement, manufacturer's address, and proper listing of ingredients. When there are health risks from an ingredient or additive in a pet food, the FDA asks for "scientific evidence" that shows that this is the case. It can then prohibit or require the manufacturers to modify an ingredient's use.

As for pet food, Ethoxyquin is often used as a preservative. Ethoxyquin can be put into the mix by a feed grain mill, a rendering plant or by a pet food company. Only if a pet food company uses Ethoxyquin does it have to be listed on the label. According to literature provided by the FDA/CVM:

> A few years ago, the center began receiving reports from dog owners attributing a myriad of adverse effects to the presence of Ethoxyquin in dog food. The reported effects include allergic reactions, skin problems, major organ failure, behavior problems and cancer. However, there is little available scientific data to support these contentions, or to show other adverse effects in dogs at levels approved for use in dog foods. As such, there is no scientific basis to warrant change in the regulatory status of Ethoxyquin at this time.[6]

In February of 1993, Carol Barfield, co-founder of the United Animal Owners Association in Cleveland, Ohio, petitioned the FDA/CVM to have Ethoxyquin removed from dog food. Months later she received a "tentative response" to the petition. The FDA/CVM claimed that the petition was deficient in that it did not provide "research data specifically on the dog species, but instead contained studies on other animal species." FDA/CVM requires "scientific evidence" that would indicate a health concern. At that time the only study in progress was being conducted by the manufacturer of this substance, Monsanto.[7]

In late 1993, because of the allegations made by breeders that related to health concerns of foods containing Ethoxyquin, Monsanto commissioned an accredited, independent laboratory to conduct a three-year study on its product. In the spring of 1996, the results of this study were disclosed. The study, a feeding trial, was conducted on Beagles (the breed of choice for testers). One group was fed food that contained 180 to 360 parts per million (ppm) of Ethoxyquin. According to *Petfood Industry* magazine:

> **Consistent with previous work, the researchers noted liver pigmentation changes and elevated liver enzymes that depended on the dosage of Ethoxyquin. The minimal liver pigmentation that occurred at 180 ppm, in females, was not considered clinically significant because there were no liver enzyme changes or associated pathological changes in the liver or other organs. In addition the dogs' overall health was not affected.[8]**

Monsanto shared the results of this study with the FDA and requested "FDA's independent verification of Monsanto's conclusion." (Monsanto also manufactures the bovine growth hormone (BGH), another product that has elicited much controversy. To date it is still banned from a number of countries including Canada but has been in use in the United States since late 1993.)

The second case that the FDA/CVM describes in its literature concerns propylene glycol, a humectant used in semi-moist pet food. Propylene glycol has been proven to be a major contributor in feline cardiac disease set forth in scientifically sound studies accepted by the FDA. The FDA publication, "Understanding Pet Food Labels," states:

> **It [propylene glycol] was known to cause overt anemia or other clinical effects. However, recent reports of scientifically sound studies show that propylene glycol reduces red blood cell survival time, renders red blood cells more susceptible to oxidative damage, and has other adverse effects in cats consuming the substance at levels found in semi-moist foods.[9]**

This humectant is also used in semi-moist dog foods but apparently no "scientifically sound studies" have shown adverse effect in dogs.

At the time of this writing, the FDA/CVM has managed to prohibit the use of propylene glycol in semi-moist cat food. Propylene glycol was in semi-moist cat food for approximately fifteen years. This substance is a second cousin to antifreeze. How many cats have suffered the consequences of this substance? How many thousands, if not millions of dollars have been spent on veterinary bills to treat the illnesses caused by propylene glycol?

If your dog or cat becomes ill after eating a pet food manufactured in the United States, can you go to the FDA/CVM and request that they investigate? Basically, no, unless you can provide scientific data that indicates the source of the problem. Then, and only then, will the FDA investigate.

The FDA/CVM focuses on health claims made by pet food companies, especially if they are labeled for the prevention or treatment of a disease. In 1990 some pet food manufacturers advertised that their cat food might prevent Feline Urological Syndrome (FUS). This is a drug claim. The companies were given ample time to change these labels and when some did not comply, the FDA and state officials seized hundreds of tons of cat food. One company, whose products were seized, assured the FDA that the product would no longer be labeled for the prevention of FUS and sold in the United States. This does not mean that they cannot continue to sell it in countries without legislation— Canada, for one.

The Association of American Feed Control Officials (AAFCO) is a national organization of federal and state officials that regulate label text, ingredient definitions, and product names. Its canine and feline "nutrient profiles" are primarily nutrient minimums with maximums stated. Manufacturers of pet food are only required to comply with the regulations, if any, of their particular state or the state in which the product is being sold.

The AAFCO has no enforcement authority. This organization does not undertake any analytical testing on pet food nor does it determine the sources of protein, fiber, or fats, used in the product. It does provide an extensive list of "ingredient definitions," which gives a wide leeway for the pet food industry to use the cheapest ingredients available.[10] Again, if a particular state adopts the AAFCO guidelines, they must also adhere to the ingredient definitions. As discussed in previous chapters, we have seen what some of those ingredients consist of.

In my questionnaire, sent to each state in the United States, I asked five questions, in addition to the question asked on the rendering of companion animals. (See Chapter Two for answers to my question, "Does your state prohibit the use of rendered companion animals in pet food?")

Question One: *"Could you please advise if your state adheres to the AAFCO guidelines regarding pet food ingredients?"*
Twenty states replied; out of those, thirteen stated that they adhere to AAFCO guidelines. Alaska and Florida have no regulations at all.[11] Since not all states replied these may be states where no regulations exist.

Question Two: *"Would testing be undertaken by your state officials to ascertain the sources of protein used in pet food?"*
Not one of the twenty states that replied undertakes any kind of testing; nor does one inquire as to the sources of proteins used in pet foods.

Question Three: *"Would testing be undertaken as to the quality of grains and fats used?*
Again the reply was the same as to question two. The excuses for lack of testing were: manpower shortage, lack of funding and equipment.

Question Four: *"Do you test to ascertain the levels of bacteria, pesticides, drugs, and heavy metals in the raw material used in pet foods?"*
The replies to this question were wide and varied. Eighteen of the twenty states undertook no testing at all. Two states (New York and Massachusetts) wrote that their feed and food laboratories had the facilities to check for drug residue, but that financial and personnel constraints limited any testing to an "as needed" basis. Two states (Idaho and Oregon) advised that they test for drug residue in livestock feed but not in pet food. In reading the various state "Commercial Feed Laws," there is nothing that would indicate pet food must be tested for any pathogen or toxin.

There are about 250 rendering companies in the United States. According to the National Renderers Association, which has about 130 members, 92 percent of the production of animal protein such as meat and bone meal, is tested for *Salmonella* contamination. The Animal Protein Producers Industry is a voluntary program that mandates *Salmonella* testing to maintain membership in their organization.[12] When I contacted one of the largest rendering facilities in the United States, I was advised that testing for *Salmonella* is undertaken on a monthly basis.[13] This particular facility advised that no testing is conducted for drug residue in rendered material.

According to the "Pet Food Rules and Regulations," as provided by some of the states replying to my questionnaire, labels must contain the following: guaranteed analysis, ingredient statement, (the ingredient statement does not disclose the levels of drugs, etcetera., which may be contained therein), brand name of the product, moisture content, and identification of the producer.[14] The above information must be shown on the label. If it is a medicated food, this information must also appear. This all looks impressive when you consider that the FDA/CVM, and the AAFCO, an association of governmental officers, are involved. However, looks can be deceiving.

Labels are supposed to provide us with all the information we require to make an informed decision on the appropriate food for our pet. However, ingredient statements in pet food disclose only vague information and terms, such as meat meal, meat by-products, digest, and tankage. Labels do not disclose the actual species of animal these are derived from.

In 1996, *Cats* magazine published an article by the president of AAFCO, Roger Hoestenbach. In it, he stated that the number-one reason why "exact ingredients" are not listed is because of label space.[15] How much more label space would it take to eliminate "meat meal" and give us the exact source of this meat meal; such as kangaroo, raccoon, diseased cattle tissue, chicken feet, dogs, or cats. In human food, if the product contains chicken, it is so stated. If the product is a meat pie you will find the kind of meat on the label—not so with pet food.

The FDA/CVM and the AAFCO are supposedly interested in the accurate labeling of pet food. We are made aware of the percentage of protein, fat, carbohydrates, and moisture that are in these products but we have no indication if they provide the nutrition our pets require. Dr. David Bebiak, Director of Pet Nutrition and Care Research at Ralston Purina Co., states in *The Pet Dealer*, "The purpose of pet food labels is to provide consumers with information that helps them select the best for their pets."[16] We rely on the pet food industry to tell us that this is the "best food for our pets." We assume that the FDA/CVM is like a responsible parent overseeing the ingredients used in these foods, investigating if there was a complaint. We assume incorrectly.

Recently, I asked a U.S. veterinarian, "If I suspect that a pet food caused an illness in my pets, to whom would I state my concerns?" Her reply was, "The pet food company that manufactured the food." Perhaps I should have regaled her with my experience with the company whose food made my dogs ill. Complaining to the company is like handing the fox the keys to the chicken house.

Basically, in the United States and in Canada there are no regulations. Canadians have been lulled into believing that government and voluntary organizations are overseeing every ingredient in a can or bag of pet food. One U.S. state official to whom I expressed my concerns about the lack of regulations in Canada was very open with his comments: "I am not sure that Canada is worse off then the United States for not having regulations." He went on to write:

> **Making sure pet food is sufficiently nutritious does not necessarily insure the dog or cat is properly nourished, however. The pet would also have to be fed the pet food at proper intervals and fed only the pet food, no table scraps or other supplements detracting from a balanced diet. The regulations do, however, encourage prospective owners into believing they can properly nourish their cat or dog without much thought, which encourages citizens to own more pets, and promotes the sale of more pet food. If I were to give the primary purpose for the regulations, I would say it is to promote the sale of pet food.[17]**

As I began my search for answers after my pets became ill, I found that the only Canadian government regulations of pet food falls under the Labelling Act. The label must contain the name and address of the company, weight of the product, and if it is produced for dog or cat. No other information is required.

When I began meeting with Canadian government officials, most were shocked that no regulations existed. And as The Honorable Tom Hockin so aptly put it, "They [the pet food industry] must have fallen through the cracks."[18] All promised to investigate and contact the appropriate government department. Their investigation entailed asking someone if regulations existed and passing the buck on to another department. Not one government official pursued this issue until Ontario's Provincial Minister of Agriculture, The Honorable Elmer Buchanan, decided to set up a committee to investigate.

I spent one year working with this committee looking at the industry in the United States and the United Kingdom. My hope was that somehow the government would see fit to at least regulate the ingredients used in pet food. One year later a decision was arrived at—the provincial government was not in a position to regulate this industry. It must be a federal matter.[19] Previously, I had contacted our federal government only to be told that they felt that the two voluntary organizations, the Canadian Veterinary Medical Association (CVMA) and the Pet Food Association of Canada (PFAC), were doing an adequate job. (These organizations will be discussed at greater length later in this chapter.)

In 1992 we had an election and a new Minister of Agriculture had been appointed, The Honorable Charles Meyer. At this point I felt that it was worth one more try. Needless to say, I was rather surprised to receive a letter asking if I would be willing to work with a representative from his staff in order to "find a mutually acceptable solution to this problem."[20]

Lengthy discussions would lead to a compromise—voluntary controls overseen by government. Voluntary controls were not what I wanted, but at least it was a starting point. Six months passed and I heard nothing. I was cognizant that meetings between government and the pet food industry were being held and I was eager to ascertain the outcome. Finally a reply came from veterinarian I. Kirk, assistant to Charles Meyer. Andre Gravel, the veterinarian from the ministry, with whom I had worked, was no longer there. Yes, the meetings had been held and the industry wanted to see "more structure in the labeling of pet food products."[21] They wanted to see standards or rules for the labeling of pet food which would allow declarations such as "new," "improved," "high digestibility." None of these smoke and mirrors had anything to do with the heart of the problem—the ingredients. The letter ended, "given the current environment of government restructuring and fiscal restraint, I honestly cannot predict a fast and speedy resolution to this issue." I interpreted this response to mean that the government would do nothing.

Fed up with government bureaucracy, I contemplated if I should even bother contacting our new Minister of Agriculture, The Honorable Ralph Goodale. Like numerous other politicians, he felt that the voluntary organizations were doing an adequate job. He wrote to me as follows: "However, it is clear that the safety of animal food products is the responsibility of industry. Under these circumstances, the Department may elect to audit the delivery to standards. I would anticipate that any resource implication for the delivery of pet food control programs would be the responsibility of industry."[22] I queried as to what other food-related industry is allowed to regulate itself. His next letter ignored my query and like his predecessors, referred to the CVMA and its voluntary regulations. He also advised that Industry Canada (Consumer and Corporate Affairs), not only regulates labeling but also investigates consumer complaints.[23]

"Investigate consumer complaints." This was the first time that I was aware that a government agency might become involved if a problem existed with a commercial pet food. Immediately, I contacted the Minister of Industry Canada, The Honorable Ralph Manley, requesting specific information on this regulation. His reply: "While I appreciate your concerns, I must advise you that there is no authority under the Consumer Packaging and Labelling Act nor any other legislation administered by Industry Canada to regulate the quality and safety of pet food sold in Canada."[24]

Every pet owner to whom I speak is positive that the government regulates this industry. A pet-supply store owner became incensed when I advised him that this was an unregulated industry. He was convinced that Agriculture Canada inspected every piece of meat and grain put into pet food.

After five years, I finally gave up dealing with Canadian politicians. The Canadian government was simply not going to regulate this industry. The pet food industry does not want regulations and the government is not about to ruffle the feathers of this corporate giant.

As previously mentioned, we have two voluntary organizations in Canada that purportedly oversee pet food made in Canada. Both the CVMA and PFMA set voluntary guidelines. However, voluntary guidelines cannot be enforced. The CVMA undertakes "digestibility feeding trials" for the foods it endorses. These feeding trials, like the ones in the United States, run for not more than twenty-six weeks.[25] As a pet owner for thirty years, I am aware that feeding problems may not occur for months or even a few years after a pet has been on a particular food. Kidney, liver, and heart disease, cancer and other internal problems may be developing and are not immediately discernible.

Twenty-six weeks cannot accurately indicate the long-term effect the food might have on a dog or cat.

Another requirement for certification by the CVMA is that the food must be palatable. CVMA tests pet food for its nutritional value and levels of nutrient digestibility. Again, as with the United States, no testing is undertaken to ascertain sources of protein, carbohydrates, or fats. No testing is undertaken for levels of pathogens, drugs, pesticides, or heavy metals. If any testing is done for drug residues it is conducted by the manufacturer, not the CVMA.

Participating companies are asked to sign a "voluntary declaration" that states that the meat used comes from government-inspected plants.[26] This notion of "government-inspected plants" can be troublesome. Yes, the meat may be from government-inspected plants. Yes, the meat may be government inspected. But what they neglect to mention is that the meat from these slaughterhouses, destined for pet food, has been designated by the inspector as "unfit for human consumption." This can include lungs, bowels, digestive tracts, and euthanized pets, or it can be diseased and contaminated material—only the meat inspector knows.

In 1989 the cost to have a pet food certified by the CVMA ran between $8,000 and $15,000 (Canadian). This cost covered plant inspection, digestibility trials, and chemical analysis. Subsequent plant inspections and lab fees are estimated to be $5,000 to $8,000 per formula, per year. None of the large multinational companies are involved in these voluntary programs in Canada. For the most part, the products that are certified by the CVMA are house brands and generic products.

In 1993 a colleague questioned a source of protein used in one of the foods certified by the CVMA. She contacted its Ottawa office and expressed her concern. She requested that the CVMA investigate and contact her. Instead of dealing with the issue, the CVMA turned the information over to the company involved and asked that it deal with it. This organization purports to act as a "third party," supposedly an unbiased third party, but the methods used in the case of complaints, does not support this theory.

The Pet Food Association of Canada (PFAC) is the second voluntary organization in Canada. To date I have not seen a pet food that bears its certification logo. As with the CVMA, no testing is undertaken by PFAC to ascertain the sources of protein used in the foods that it certifies. PFAC feels that self-regulation is more acceptable than government or third-party intervention. As part of its consumer advertising literature in 1990, it stated that PFAC would provide government officials with a current list of participating products for the monitoring of product and label claims.[27]

In March of 1995, I contacted both the Federal and Provincial Ministries of Agriculture and under the "Freedom of Information Act," requested that they provide a copy of the list submitted to them by PFAC.[28] Both ministries replied that they had never been provided with such a list by PFAC. Five years after the literature was available, PFAC had not provided either branches of the government with this list. Undaunted, I contacted PFAC, and asked if such a list existed. The reply I received was short and to the point, "As of this date, no list of products approved under the PFAC Nutrition Assurance Program has been issued."[29] I wonder how many people read this literature and assumed that the government was monitoring the products certified by PFAC?

In January 1993, *The Toronto Star* printed an article I had written regarding the inferior ingredients used in commercial pet foods. In this article, I described the sources of meat meal and the quality of grains and fats. Shortly after the article appeared, I surreptitiously acquired a letter that the manager of PFAC sent to the newspaper. He wrote that I "totally misrepresented the high standards adhered to by our industry."[30] His letter went on to explain how the industry is very concerned about the health of our pets but he chose not to address the pertinent issue—the sources of ingredients used in these foods. His letter was never published by *The Toronto Star*.

So what regulations do we have in Canada? None. No federal or provincial legislation. The two voluntary organizations cater to the industry, not the consumers. What is needed, in both the United States and Canada, are government-enforced regulations of this industry.

Until then, *Buyer Beware*.

Chapter Seven

Recipes and Other Helpful Hints for a Healthy Pet

We have seen what is used in commercial pet foods, yet again and again we are warned by the pet food industry and many veterinarians that human food should never be fed to our pets. However, I am not placing all veterinarians in the same category. Over the last seven years I have encountered many wonderful veterinarians who recommend that we avoid commercial foods and opt for a homemade diet. Drs. Wendell Belfield, Richard Pitcairn, Alfred Plechner, Tom Lonsdale, and no doubt many more across the country all state that pets enjoy a much healthier and longer life if we take the time to cook for them. Dr. Wendell Belfield states in his book, *How to Have a Healthier Dog*:

> **What's wrong with carrots and peas and salad and even fruits and cooked cereal? Nothing that I know of. I know a retired veterinarian in his eighties who has been feeding generations of dogs from table scraps. Meat, vegetables, grains, fruit. His dogs were rarely ill.[1]**

The pet food industry has been in existence for more than one hundred years, but has only gained real success since the 1950s. America's food giants found a lucrative market for disposal of their by-products. Both cereal manufacturers and meat packers jumped on the bandwagon. Small pet food companies were soon gobbled up by corporate giants. By the mid-1970s pet food began to imitate human food in appearance. Pet food burgers resembling real hamburger, meat balls in gravy (a concoction described as stew), and the latest, pasta. These humanized foods are designed to appeal to owners more than the pet.

Now in the 1990s, some pet food manufacturers advertise "all natural" food to cater to health conscious pet owners. Most contain the same dubious ingredients as the rest. For those of us born before the 1950s, many of us remember that our pets were fed dinner leftovers. There was never any concern that they were not getting the right balance of protein, fats, and carbohydrates. If we ate the food, we figured it was good enough for our dogs and cats.

Some orthodox veterinarians state that in the old days our pets were not really healthier on a homemade diet. Their position is that veterinarians did not have the technology to diagnose the many diseases we see in our pets today. If that was the case, our pets should have been dying at a much younger age. My personal experience, and those of friends and colleagues, is that most of our animals used to live to a ripe old age.

How well versed are most veterinarians on the nutritional aspect of pet health? I have queried a number of veterinary colleges and have found that they provide a short course, usually a week or two, over the four or five years a student attends veterinary school. Most of these nutrition courses are taught by a nutritionist from a pet food company! Veterinary colleges also receive grants from the pet food industry. Many of these veterinarians, who have little knowledge of canine and feline nutrition, are also selling these foods in their practice. Of course, before a clinic will sell these foods, a company representative will give them a short course outlining the complete and balanced virtues of the food.

In 1995 journalist and animal lover, Catherine O'Driscoll, with her husband John Watt, a systems analyst, conducted a survey for their *Canine Health Census*. One hundred twenty-six dogs were fed a homemade diet for six months or longer and the results were astounding. The visible changes included more energy and activity, improved teeth and gums, skin, weight, and behavioral improvements. Other benefits reported included lower susceptibility to fleas, improved appetite, absence of stomach and digestive upsets, cleaner ears, and 73 percent reduction in veterinary visits. Dogs put on the homemade diet for even a few weeks showed improvement.[2]

When my dogs became ill after eating the commercial food, they were immediately switched to a human food diet. Our own veterinarian, although not familiar with feeding human food to dogs and cats, felt that this was a safe alternative to commercial food. My sister has also become dedicated to cooking for her dog. Punkie experienced numerous skin problems. Drugs would eliminate the problem for a short time, but as soon as the drugs were withdrawn, the rashes would soon return. Since she began feeding Punkie a homemade diet more than five years ago, the problems have resolved themselves.

Although cooking for your pet takes a little extra time the results are well worth it. One friend who raises German Shepherds cooks for nearly fifty dogs on a daily basis. She would never go back to using commercial pet food.

Over the years, the one thing that I have learned is that many people are terrified to feed their pet anything other than what comes out of a can or bag. They believe that their pet will keel over and die. I suggest to any pet owner whose pet has a serious health problem to first consult a holistic or naturopathic veterinarian, and then try feeding your pet a homemade diet.

I have attempted to provide a diet for my pets that incorporates all the protein, carbohydrates, fiber, and fats that they require. Much controversy revolves around the cooking and not cooking of the protein matter.[3] Because I have been so deeply involved with all aspects of the meat industry, including conditions at some slaughterhouses, I *always* cook the meat for my guys. In cooking the meat, you are destroying some of the healthy enzymes, but you are also destroying bacteria and parasites.

When arguing this issue with people who are very much opposed to cooking meat, the topic always reverts to dogs in the wild. "Dogs in the wild don't sit around and cook their prey." I argue that the prey of dogs in the wild usually does not contain high levels of drugs, hormones, heavy metals, pesticides, and so on, which cooking, to some extent, destroys. In addition, dogs and cats today are usually raised on cooked, processed and extruded commercial foods and their systems just cannot handle raw meat. Some people advise to feed only organically raised meat and grains, not only for health reasons, but for humane treatment of the farm animals raised for food. Unless you can afford organically raised meat and grains or free-range chickens, I recommend always cooking any meat fed to companion animals.

Although both dogs and cats are carnivores, cats require much more protein than dogs; and kittens require more protein than a full-grown cat. Dogs can subsist on a vegetarian diet, but cats require a meat source of protein. Vegetable protein does not contain all the amino acids that are required; therefore, a correct formulation of grains and other ingredients must be made if you plan on feeding your dog a vegetarian diet.

Indigestible proteins, such as those used in some commercial foods (hair, feathers, fecal matter), cannot sustain an animal. Meat, fish, eggs (a complete source of protein), and dairy products provide many, if not all, the amino acids that your pet requires. Carbohydrates and fiber come primarily from grains and vegetables and provide energy and stamina and also provide calories to maintain weight. Grains should be cooked, and vegetables, steamed or raw, should be finely chopped. In this form grains and vegetables are more easily eaten.

Sunflower, corn, and safflower oil provide your pet with added energy, a lush coat, clear skin, and good muscle tone. I usually use safflower oil in the diet I prepare for my cats. In commercial pet food, hair, peanut hulls, beet pulp and even ground up paper can be used as sources of fiber. Pets eating a homemade diet obtain their fiber primarily from the vegetables and fruit. As two of my cats are rather old and prone to constipation, I often add a teaspoon of natural bran to their food. My pets eat three meals a day: breakfast, lunch, and dinner. However, many pet owners feed their pets two meals per day.

Some nutritionists advise that pets should not eat protein, carbohydrates (grains) and vegetables at the same meal. Their reasoning is that when proteins and carbohydrates are ingested together, the protein is digested first, leaving the carbohydrates to digest later. Toxins are released due to the fermentation of the carbohydrates.[4] The ideal diet would include feeding meat or dairy products that can be combined with vegetables at one meal. Grains mixed with fruits and vegetables can be served at the next meal. I assume that this applies to dogs as I just can't see my cats sitting down to a meal of grains and fruits or vegetables. Pat Lazarus, animal nutritionist, recommends in *Keep Your Pet Healthy the Natural Way*, "The only harmonious foods to be used with meats or even dairy proteins are vegetables (raw and grated or cut up)."[5] However, my own personal experience is that I have always fed protein, carbohydrates, and fruits or vegetables together. This has never caused any problem with any of my animals.

Much is not known about a nutrition and a balanced diet for pets. The diet for my dog is based on my own years of experience cooking for my animals, as well as extensive information gathering. The following suggestions are not based on scientific evidence, but rather accumulated knowledge and sound advice from veterinarians who know more about nutrition than I do. The diet for my dog includes:

⅓ PROTEIN—either meat (beef, chicken, turkey, lamb), fish or eggs. Some dogs are allergic to eggs. If you serve pork be sure that it is well cooked.

⅓ CARBOHYDRATES—either brown rice (well-cooked), oatmeal, pasta, mashed potatoes, shredded wheat or other whole grain cereals, whole grain breads, plain or toasted. There is an array of grains to choose from, just be sure that they are well cooked for proper digestion.

⅓ VEGETABLES OR FRUITS—carrots, zucchini, yams, sweet potatoes, peas, yellow and green beans, mushrooms, apples, pears, watermelon— just about any fruit. Small amounts of cabbage, broccoli, and brussels sprouts can be used, but these vegetables tend to cause gas.

VEGETABLE OIL—Depending on the size of the dog, one teaspoon to one tablespoon, per day of vegetable oil.

For breakfast, my dog gets a bowl of oatmeal with a small amount of meat or fruit mixed in. Lunch and dinner are composed of meat, grains, and fruit or vegetables. With either lunch or dinner I add a tablespoon of yogurt or cottage cheese (calcium). Both the dogs and cats enjoy a treat of bean sprouts, parsley, or alfalfa. These are sources of many minerals, vitamin C, and fiber.

My brother decided to feed his dog a homemade diet, only his dog disliked the carbohydrates and fiber aspect of this diet. The dog's favorite meat was liver. At mealtime, the dog would pick out the liver and leave the rest. Needless to say after a week of eating just liver, the dog had severe diarrhea. If your dog picks out just certain ingredients, try putting it in a blender and chopping it all together. This makes it rather difficult for them to pick out what they like and leave the rest!

Some experts say that it is not necessary to add supplements if you are providing your pet with a healthy, balanced diet of protein, grains, fiber, and fats. Others advise that to be on the safe side, a multi-vitamin and mineral can be added. These can be purchased at a pet shop or through your veterinarian.

One supplement of particular value is vitamin C. Nutritional veterinarians have found that although dogs and cats produce vitamin C, any stress, illness, or infection depletes their supply of vitamin C. This vitamin keeps the immune system healthy, thus preventing bacterial infection.[6] As dogs age, their production of vitamin C diminishes. Dr. Wendell Belfield has written extensively on the use of vitamin C for arthritic and degenerative diseases and the wonderful results that are obtained by adding this to the pet's diet. Dr. Belfield recommends the following dosage of vitamin C:[7]

SMALL DOGS	500 TO 1,500 MG.
MEDIUM DOGS	1,500 TO 3,000 MG.
LARGE DOGS	3,000 TO 6,000 MG.
GIANT DOGS	6,000 TO 7,500 MG.

My Newfoundland, the giant breed, takes about 3,000 mg. of vitamin C per day. This is somewhat lower than Dr. Belfield suggests, but my dog develops loose stools if I go much higher. I began by giving him 1,000 mg. per day and increased the dosage slowly. I use powdered calcium ascorbate as a vitamin C source because it is easier on the dog's stomach. If you are giving a multi-vitamin and mineral supplement, additional vitamin C may be required.

The other vitamin that I have given my dog for the past three years is vitamin E. This has brought him renewed vitality. His morning stiffness disappeared shortly after the addition of vitamin E, and according to Dr. Belfield, "It boosts the efficiency of the heart and the circulatory system."[8] Dr. Belfield also writes, "Along with rejuvenating action on the cardiovascular system, vitamin E has another unique quality that appears to slow down aging. It is a natural antioxidant." Dr. Belfield recommends the following dose of vitamin E, which is always measured in international units (IU).

SMALL DOGS	100 IU
MEDIUM DOGS	200 IU
LARGE DOGS	200 IU
GIANT DOGS	400 IU

Charlie receives 200 IU in the form of d-alpha tocopherol. There is no doubt in my mind that the natural diet and the supplements have added years to Charlie's life and kept him in good health. Charlie is a Newfoundland, and the average life span of this breed is eight years, however, Charlie is fourteen years old as of 1997.

Feeding cats a natural diet can be a little more complex, especially if they have been fed commercial foods for most of their lives. Be assured it can be done, and they will enjoy their new diet just as much as the dog does.

Cats require more protein than dogs; therefore, their diet should be comprised of $2/3$ meat and $1/3$ grain and vegetables or fruit. Chicken and turkey seem to be the favorites with my four cats, although every so often I open a can of salmon and they go wild. Fish of any kind is low in vitamin E, and vitamin E is required in high amounts by cats, so too much fish is not a good idea. Perhaps once a week you can give your cat some fish, which provides polyunsaturated fats that your cat cannot obtain from meat.

All meals for my cats are composed of protein, carbohydrates, and fiber plus a teaspoon of vegetable oil per day. This is all processed in the blender, but I hold back a few chunks of meat and add it to their food. This gives them something to chew on.

You can purchase a vitamin and mineral supplement from your veterinarian or pet store if you feel that your cats are not getting all the nutrients they require.

Fiber, in the form of natural bran, can be added. One half to one teaspoon if your cat suffers from constipation. Constipation is a frequent problem in older cats. To help this, make sure that water is always available for your pet.

Despite what many veterinarians tell us about the problems encountered when we give our pets milk, I have given both my dog and cats milk (2 percent) for many years and none have developed diarrhea. The two Siamese prefer water but will drink milk once in a while.

Anyone starting their pet on a natural diet should do it gradually. Begin by mixing a small amount of the new food into the food they have been eating. Increase the amount of the new diet until they are completely switched over.

You will notice that when you are feeding a natural diet, your pets will be producing far fewer stools. When I was feeding commercial foods to my dogs, I was cleaning up the yard three or four times a day. After switching to a natural diet, once a day was the maximum. I thought perhaps something was lacking in their natural diet. Our veterinarian assured me that the reason for the decline in stools was that the dogs were absorbing the food they were eating; the food was not going straight through the digestive system as the commercial food had.

Dental health is another concern for pet owners. Although my dog is fourteen years old, his teeth are in perfect condition. Twice a week I drag a marrow bone out of the freezer, let it thaw, and give it to him. Cats also enjoy chewing on bones. If you have a dog that is a voracious chewer, give him a knuckle bone. This will keep him occupied for hours. (See end of chapter, Rawhide Bones, for discussion on bones.)

Examining the diet of dogs in the wild after they killed their prey it was found that they also ate the prey's stomach contents of vegetables, grains, and berries. Often the prey were herbivores that digested strictly plant matter. Grains contain nutrients not found in meat and provide sources of energy for the animals.

As for cats, their diet should also contain grain and vegetable matter. I think it still gets back to the fact that our pets are not wild animals. Most cats do not go out daily and kill their prey. Most have been fed the processed commercial food from the time they were kittens.

In the last few years, more and more concerned pet owners have decided to go that extra step and cook for their pets. However, they have been convinced that if they are going to feed a homemade diet they must add all these exotic substances. I received a brochure from a California company that sells an extensive list of compounds that states what must be added if one feeds a natural diet to a dog or cat. To purchase all the ingredients would have been costly.

Remember, our pets are the descendants of dogs and cats who, twenty or thirty years ago, ate table scraps and ravaged garbage cans. No, I don't purport to feed my animals table scraps nor do I let them raid the garbage, but I do provide, what I consider, a well-balanced diet. They have eaten this diet for more than seven years without any of these exotic ingredients, and all have done very well. Many other pet owners I know have also fed their companion animals in the same way and have healthy pets. We must be doing something right.

Photo: Sumner W. Fowler

RECIPES

Over the years, I have acquired a number of recipes for both dogs and cats, some of which you might enjoy preparing for your pet. Pets are like people, they enjoy variety. Pets are also unique individuals. To be sure they are receiving a balanced homemade diet, it would be wise to consult a holistic veterinarian who can make suggestions as to the addition or elimination of ingredients in the diet. Keep in mind that these recipes are not based on scientific studies, but rather on information and common sense gathered during the past seven years.

Most of these recipes are made in bulk or for one or two dogs. Use as little or as much as your dog requires, depending on size. Beef, chicken, turkey, and lamb can be cut into chunks or you can purchase the ground meat. Cook the meat. Fish and eggs are also cooked or steamed. Once a week, liver, kidney or tripe, all cooked, can be served.

Any grains or pasta must be cooked for proper digestion. Vegetables and fruit can be served raw although some pets prefer them steamed. Chop finely or run them through a mincer.

DOG RECIPES

RISE AND SHINE

3 cups cooked oatmeal

2 cups cooked ground beef

2 tablespoons plain yogurt

1 small apple cup in small pieces

Mix together and serve.

This meal can be served at breakfast, lunch or dinner.

SUMMER BREAKFAST

4 cups crisp rice cereal

2 scrambled eggs

1 cup grated parsnips

1 tablespoon vegetable oil

Sprinkle with 1 teaspoon brewer's yeast

Mix together and serve.

HIGH FIBER BREAKFAST

2 cups of all-bran cereal

2 tablespoons vegetable oil

1 cup cooked chicken

Top with alfalfa sprouts

Mix together and serve.

YUMMY OMELET

Fry two eggs in two tablespoons of vegetable oil

Top with bean sprouts and grated cheese
Serve.

MACARONI, LIVER, AND VEGGIE DINNER

2 cups of elbow macaroni, cooked

2 pieces of beef liver cooked in butter or oil

1 can of mixed vegetables, drained

Chop liver slices in pieces. Add macaroni and vegetables

Sprinkle with garlic powder (not garlic salt)

Serve.

MEAT, POTATOES, AND VEGETABLES

2 cups leftover mashed potatoes

1 pound ground chicken, fried

1 cup grated carrots

3 tablespoons cottage cheese

Mix potatoes, ground chicken, and grated carrots together.

Heat in individual muffin tins (Microwave 3 minutes, oven 10 minutes)

Cool and top with 1 to 3 tablespoons cottage cheese

SOMETHING FISHY

1 medium-size can of salmon, leave bones in as
they provide calcium

1 cup cooked brown rice

1 medium zucchini, grated or finely chopped

1 tablespoon wheat germ

Mix together and serve

HOLIDAY DINNER

2 cups leftover turkey

2 cups leftover mashed potatoes

1 pear, diced or chopped (pretend it is cranberries)

1 tablespoon sesame seeds

Mix together and drizzle with 2 tablespoons of yogurt.

CHINESE STYLE DINNER

2 cups of cooked brown rice

1 cup cooked ground chicken

1 cup grated carrots, zucchini, or celery

Mix together, add 1 tablespoon vegetable oil and top with alfalfa sprouts.

Fish Patties

Note: This recipe is high in protein so if your pet is on a low-protein diet, avoid this recipe.

1 15 oz. can of salmon, mackerel or other fish
3 tablespoons of parsley
2 eggs
1/2 cup whole wheat bread crumbs
Whole wheat flour
Vegetable oil for frying

Drain fish. Mix in parsley, eggs, and bread crumbs. Form into patties and roll in flour. Fry in oil until brown on both sides.

Chicken Salad

2 cups cooked, cubed chicken or 2 cups cooked ground chicken
3/4 cups chopped celery
3/4 cups chopped apples
1 cup cooked brown rice
1/2 cup plain yogurt

Mix all ingredients together and serve. Your dog might like to share this with you.

Doggie Pot Roast

1 3 or 4 pound cheap cut of beef, cut in pieces
2 large potatoes cut in pieces
2 carrots cut in pieces
1 cup green beans
1/2 teaspoon garlic powder
1 cup tomato or V-8 juice

Place all ingredients in slow cooker for approximately 5 or 6 hours or until vegetables are tender. Cool and serve.

SPAGHETTI WITH MEAT SAUCE

8 oz. whole wheat spaghetti cooked and drained
1 lb. hamburger fried
4 medium mushrooms cut in pieces
1 medium tomato, chopped
1/2 cup tomato juice

Mix hamburger with mushrooms, celery and chopped tomato.
Stir in tomato juice. Pour over spaghetti and serve warm.

ALLERGY DIET

1 lb. ground lamb
2 cup cooked brown rice
1/2 cup chopped parsley
1 cup grated zucchini
1/2 cup of plain yogurt
Fry lamb in two tablespoons of oil or steam
Add rice, parsley, zucchini.
Just before serving mix in 1/2 cup of yogurt.

ICE FRUIT POPS

Pour apple juice, peach juice or even lemonade, into ice fruit
pop containers. Freeze. Let him lick them or drop them into his bowl
of water on a hot day.

LIGHT DIET

If your dog has undergone surgery or is recovering from an illness this
is easy on the stomach.
2 cups of cooked cream of wheat
1 soft boiled egg
1 tablespoon vegetable oil.
3/4 cup grated parsnips
1/4 cup alfalfa sprouts

Mix together and serve warm

UNDER THE WEATHER
2 cups of cooked cream of wheat
1 cup plain yogurt
3 tablespoons liquid honey
1 cup of cooked, chopped chicken livers.

Mix together and serve warm

LIQUID DIET
1 cup chicken stock
1 teaspoon garlic powder
1/2 cup plain yogurt
1 tablespoon melted butter
1/2 cup finely chopped alfalfa sprouts

Combine all ingredients and serve warm.

YUMMY DESSERT
2 very ripe bananas, mashed
1/2 cup plain yogurt
2 tablespoons honey

Combine ingredients in a blender. Whip and refrigerate until ready to feed. Makes an enjoyable treat and provides a good source of calcium and potassium.

KITTY MENUS
As I mentioned previously, cats require more protein than a dog. Cats also choose one or two diets they like and tend to ignore other foods when offered.

UP AND AT IT
2 medium eggs
1 tablespoon of milk
3 tablespoons of cottage cheese
2 tablespoons of finely chopped alfalfa sprouts
Mix all ingredients together. Pour into a hot pan with a tablespoon of vegetable oil or butter. When brown on the bottom, turn and brown the other side. Chop into pieces and serve.

CHICKEN, RICE, AND VEGETABLES

2 cups of ground or chopped chicken, cooked
1 cup of cooked brown rice
1/4 cup grated carrots

Put chicken, brown rice and carrots in blender and mix well.
If there is any fat from the chicken, pour about two teaspoons over the
mix. Serve at room temperature.

LIVER FEAST

2 cups chopped beef or chicken liver
2 tablespoons of vegetable oil
1 shredded Wheat
1/4 cup grated zucchini

Cook liver in vegetable oil and chop finely
Crush Shredded Wheat. Add the grated zucchini. Serve warm.

TUNA LUNCH

Do not serve more than once a week. As we know tuna can deplete
vitamin E.
1 6 1/2 oz. can of tuna packed in oil
1/2 cup cooked brown rice
1/4 cup grated carrots
2 tablespoons of wheat germ (vitamin E)

Blend and serve at room temperature.

FELINE HASH

1 cup of regular ground hamburger
1/2 cup cooked brown rice
6 tablespoons alfalfa sprouts
3/4 cup creamed cottage cheese

Mix all ingredients together and feed at room temperature

DINNER SURPRISE

1 cup cooked or ground liver or kidney

3/4 cup cooked oatmeal

3 tablespoons grated carrots or zucchini

1/3 cup plain yogurt

3 teaspoons of butter

Mix ground meat, oatmeal and vegetables together. Melt butter and pour over mixture. Stir in yogurt and serve at room temperature.

CHICKEN STEW (FOR A CROWD)

2 pounds of chicken pieces, backs, thighs, wings. Also hearts and livers can be added.

6 slices of whole wheat bread, toasted

1/4 cup chopped parsley

1/3 cup finely chopped green beans, steamed or boiled

2 tablespoons vegetable oil.

Cook or steam the chicken until it falls off the bones and hearts and liver are tender. Discard all bones. Chop or blend together with the toast, parsley and green beans. Add vegetable oil unless there is much fat from the chicken. Leave a few pieces of chicken so there is texture in the food. Serve warm.

CHEESEBURGERS

1 cup ground beef, cooked

1/4 cup grated cheddar cheese

1/4 cup grated carrots

1 Shredded Wheat

2 tablespoons vegetable oil

Mix all ingredients together and form into patties or balls. If they do not appreciate the patties or balls, simply leave it loose.

SALMON FEAST

1 15 oz. can of salmon
1 cup cooked brown rice
1/4 cup chopped parsley or celery
3 tablespoons of plain yogurt

Drain salmon. Mix in brown rice, vegetables and yogurt.
Serve at room temperature

GET WELL TREAT

Process 1 cup of leftover beef (cooked)
1/4 cup alfalfa or parsley
1/2 cup cooked cream of wheat
1/4 cup creamed cottage cheese

Process all ingredients into a thin consistency. Serve warm.

ALLERGY DIET

2 cups ground lamb
1/2 cup grated carrots or zucchini
1 cup cooked brown rice
1/4 cup yogurt
1/4 teaspoon garlic powder

Combine all ingredients and either mix in blender or serve as is
at room temperature.

NEWBORN DIET

Should you have to feed newborn kittens, mix undiluted canned evaporated milk with a few tablespoons of plain yogurt. This mixture can be
refrigerated and warmed, as needed, at feeding time. It has also been
recommended that goat's milk is an excellent substitute.

CRUNCHIES

Perhaps your pet likes a crunchy food. These are a couple of recipes that I make and feed both the dog and cats.

1 1/2 cups whole wheat flour

1 1/2 cups rye flour

1 1/2 cups brown rice flour

1 cup wheat germ

1 teaspoon dried kelp or alfalfa

4 tablespoons vegetable oil

1 teaspoon garlic powder

1 1/4 cups beef or chicken broth or stock

Dried catnip or brewer's yeast.

Mix dry ingredients. Slowly add broth and vegetable oil. Roll out into a thin sheet. Place on cookie sheet and bake at 350 degrees until golden brown. Cool and break into bite size pieces. Toss lightly in catnip or brewer's yeast. Store in air-tight container in refrigerator.

CHICKEN CRUNCHIES

1 1/2 lbs. chicken wings, necks, backs, and liver, cooked and ground.

1 15 oz can of salmon, mackerel, or tuna in oil

1 1/2 cups rye flour

2 cups whole wheat flour

2 1/2 cups brown rice flour

1 1/2 cups wheat germ

5 tablespoons vegetable oil

2 teaspoons garlic powder

4 tablespoons powdered kelp

1 1/2 cups powdered milk

3/4 cups brewer's yeast

4 cups of beef or chicken stock

Mix dry ingredients. Mix in ground chicken and fish. Mix beef or chicken stock with vegetable oil. Blend into dry mix. Roll to 1/4" thickness and place on cookie sheet. Bake at 350 degrees until golden brown. Break into pieces. Store in air-tight container in refrigerator.

Be creative, just be sure that your pet gets the right balance of protein, carbohydrates, and fats.

VEGETARIAN DIETS

It is important to note that supplements must be added to vegetarian diets to assure that your pet is obtaining all the essential vitamins, minerals and amino acids required.

DRY MIX FOR DOGS

4 cups oats
2 cups wheat flakes or rye flakes
1 cup cracked wheat
1/2 cup whole wheat flour
1/4 cup sorghum
1/3 cup oil
1/3 cup water

Preheat oven to 275 degrees F. In large bowl combine all the dry ingredients. In a separate bowl combine all the liquid ingredients. Add the dry mix to the liquid and mix thoroughly.
Bake for one hour, stirring every 20 minutes to keep in small bits.
Serve in combination with the other dinner suggestions.

RICE-MILLET VEGETABLE DISH (TWO MEALS)

1 cup cooked rice
1 cup cooked millet
3 cups leftover vegetables
1/4 cup oil
1/2 cup water

Put the rice, millet, oil and water in a large pot. Put vegetables in blender and blend at medium speed until creamy. Add to the grains and serve warm.

ANY-KIND OF BEAN DISH

3 cups beans (pinto, limas, navy, soy, or kidney)
1/4 cup oil
1 cup cracked wheat
Combine all ingredients in large bowl. Lightly mash.

***Vegetarian Recipes are from *The Cookbook for People Who Love Animals* Published by Gentle World, Inc., P.O. Box 1418, Umatillo, FL. 32784.

VITAMINS AND MINERALS

Vitamins and minerals are as essential to the health of our companion animals as they are to human health. As with humans, it is far better to derive vitamins and minerals from the foods we eat rather than from supplements.

Commercial pet food manufacturers add vitamins and minerals as a premix. I question how heat and pressure in processing may affect the availability of these compounds? I also question if these vitamins and minerals are chelated or do they pass through the body unused if unchelated? Vitamins are essential to normal growth; they aid in the conversion of food into energy, and form a necessary part of many hormones. Vitamins C, B, and A (beta-carotene—natural form) are water-soluble vitamins, and excesses are quickly eliminated from the body. Vitamins A (retinol), D, and E are fat-soluble vitamins and remain in the body for twenty-four hours. These vitamins can become concentrated in the liver.

Minerals regulate many physiological functions such as providing oxygen to the body's cells, repair of tissue and bones and aid in the normal function of the nervous system. As little data is available on the mineral requirements of dogs and cats, information is taken from the requirements of other mammals. If you are going to supplement your pet's diet with synthetic vitamins and minerals, be sure to consult your veterinarian first. Both vitamins and minerals are required in minute amounts, hence, it is better to underdo than overdo.

VITAMIN A (BETA-CAROTENE, RETINOL)

Vitamin A-retinol is a fat-soluble vitamin and excess amounts can be toxic to humans and animals. Vitamin A maintains healthy coats and skin. promotes bone growth. protects against infection, and aids in the treatment of eye disorders. Vitamin A deficiencies result in: Night blindness, susceptibility to infections, poor growth and development, dryness, and itching.

BETA-CAROTENE is found in liver, sweet potatoes, carrots, dandelion greens (which contain five times the amount of vitamin A as carrots), apricots, broccoli, and kale.

RETINOL is found in butter, cheese, egg yolks, liver, and whole milk.

VITAMIN B-1 (THIAMINE)

The B vitamins are water-soluble but, as with all vitamins and minerals, don't go overboard. It is found in beef liver and kidneys, whole grains, bran oatmeal, salmon, wheat germ, peanuts, and kidney beans. B-1 maintains normal function of the nervous system. Works as a flea repellent. Vitamin B deficiencies may result in: unsteadiness. lesser learning ability, loss of appetite, fatigue, and vomiting.

VITAMIN B-2 (RIBOFLAVIN)

B-2 is found in cottage cheese, cheese, wheat germ, kidney, fish and chicken. It maintains healthy mucous membranes. Promotes growth and development. Contributes to healthy vision. Vitamin B-2 deficiencies may result in: cataracts, sensitivity to light, dermatitis, and weakness in the hind legs.

VITAMIN B-3 (NIACIN)

B-3 is found in beef liver, white chicken meat, peanuts, salmon, tuna, turkey, whole grains, and milk. Maintains muscle tone, healthy skin, and coat. Converts food to energy and in some cases, prevents seizures. Vitamin B-3 deficiencies may result in: blacktongue disease, muscle weakness, loss of appetite, and foul breath.

VITAMIN B-5 (PANTOTHENIC ACID)

B-5 is found in eggs, wheat germ, lentils, liver, brewer's yeast, peas, and whole grain products. Improves longevity. Aids in wound healing and protects against stress and infection. Vitamin B-5 deficiencies may result in: nervousness, loss of appetite, and fatigue.

VITAMIN B-6 (PYRIDOXINE)

B-6 is found in bananas, bran, brewer's yeast, carrots, salmon, tuna, wheat germ, lentils, and whole-grain cereals. Promotes red-blood cell formulation. Maintains a strong immune system. Contributes to a healthy nervous system. Vitamin B-6 deficiencies may result in: weakness, nervousness, slow growth, weight loss, and inflammation of the skin.

VITAMIN B-12 (CYANOCOBALAMIN)

B-12 is found in sardines, herring, milk products, eggs, organ meats, and beef. B-12 treats anemia. Promotes normal growth and development. Stimulates weight gain in puppies. Deficiencies may result in: anemia. loss of appetite, pale mucous membranes, weakness, and fatigue.

BIOTIN

Biotin is a lesser-known vitamin of the B family. It is also known as vitamin H. Biotin is found in brown rice, butter, tuna, eggs, chicken, cheese, liver, lentils, milk, and oats. Prevents skin problems. Facilitates metabolism of amino acids and carbohydrates. Promotes the health of nerve cells. Biotin deficiencies may result in: loss of appetite, anemia, and skin disorders. If the pet is on antibiotic or sulfa drugs, they may also develop a biotin deficiency.

VITAMIN C (ASCORBIC ACID)

The natural sources of vitamin C are: oranges, peppers, tomatoes, broccoli, kiwi, rose hips, strawberries, basically most fruits and vegetables supply amounts of vitamin C. Vitamin C is essential for the formation of collagen. Promotes tissue and wound healing. Prevents infection. Can detoxify foreign substances entering the blood stream. Reduces the pain of arthritis. Vitamin C deficiencies may result in: swollen or painful joints, anemia, slow healing of wounds and tissue, foul breath, and loose teeth.

VITAMIN D (CHOLECALCIFEROL)

Vitamin D is fat-soluble. Found in salmon, sardines, cod-liver oil, herring, and mackerel. Sun exposure also provides vitamin D. Works with calcium and phosphorus to promote bone and tooth formation. Vitamin D deficiencies may result in: malformation of bones and joints, and bones that break easily.

VITAMIN E (ALPHA-TOCOPHEROL)

Vitamin E is fat-soluble, found in wheat germ, whole wheat flour, margarine, corn oil, peanut oil, and eggs. Acts as an anti-blood clotting agent. Promotes muscle growth and repair. Improves the immune system. Promotes the healing of many skin problems. Improves the heart and circulatory system. Vitamin E deficiencies may result in: muscle weakness, lethargy, and lack of energy.
Note: Vitamin E acts as an antioxidant and is often used as a preservative in natural pet foods.

VITAMIN K (PHYTONADIONE)

Vitamin K is fat-soluble. Found in alfalfa, cheddar cheese, oats, spinach, and brussel sprouts. Prevents abnormal bleeding. Used in the treatment of dogs that have been poisoned with warfarin (rat poison). Deficiencies: shortages of vitamin K are rare.

MINERALS

CALCIUM AND PHOSPHORUS

These two minerals are usually considered together due to their utilization in the body. Calcium and phosphorus are found in milk, cheese, canned salmon, bone meal, legumes, meat, and eggs. Calcium provides strong bones and teeth. Helps regulate blood clotting and promotes the use of amino acids. Phosphorus, as with calcium, promotes strong bones and teeth. Calcium deficiencies may result in: brittle bones, painful joints, poor appetite, soft teeth, and receding gums. Note: Calcium and phosphorus ratios are between 1.2 to 1 and 1.4 to 1—in other words, 1.2 to 1.4 parts of calcium to 1 part of phosphorus. Both require adequate amounts of vitamin D to be used by the animal's body. Excess levels of calcium in the diet are a danger, since excess levels can cause accumulations on the bones. Kidney failure and constipation are also attributed to excess levels of calcium.

CHROMIUM

Chromium, a trace element, can be found in dairy products, seafood, whole grain products, beef, chicken, and fresh fruits. Chromium helps insulin in the regulation of blood sugar. Chromium deficiencies may result in: cloudy eye corneas and sugar in the urine.

COBALT

Cobalt is also a trace mineral that is found in liver, milk, spinach, kidney, eggs, and watercress. Promotes normal red blood cell formulation. Required for the production of vitamin B-12. Cobalt deficiencies may result in: anemia, weight loss, fatigue, and weakness.

COPPER

Natural sources include mushrooms, oats, wheat germ, black-strap molasses, salmon, and lentils. Copper promotes red blood cell formation. It is a catalyst for the storage and release of iron for the formation of hemoglobin for red blood cells. Copper deficiencies may result in: anemia, faulty collagen formation, and reproductive problems.

IODINE

Natural sources of iodine include table salt, kelp, canned salmon, cod, herring, haddock, and lobster. Promotes the normal function of the thyroid gland. Aids in normal cell function and keeps skin and coat healthy. Iodine deficiencies may result in: fatigue, sparse coat, and poor growth.

IRON

Natural sources include liver, egg yolks, wheat germ, whole grain products, cheese, black-strap molasses, lentils, and enriched bread. Prevents anemia and poor growth in puppies and forms part of the several proteins and enzymes in the body. Iron deficiencies may result in: fatigue, anemia, listlessness, and lowered resistance to disease and infections.

MAGNESIUM

Natural sources of magnesium are wheat germ, molasses, cod, carp, halibut, shrimp, green vegetables, and nuts. Aids in bone growth, and the absorption of calcium and vitamins C, E, and B complex. Promotes healthy nerves and muscles. Magnesium deficiencies may result in: skin problems, seizures, slow weight gain, and muscle weakness.

MANGANESE

Natural sources of manganese include, bran, peas, spinach, oatmeal, and seaweed. Aids in cell function. Promotes cartilage and bone growth. Manganese deficiencies may result in: poor growth, and problems of the joints and discs.

MOLYBDENUM

Natural sources of molybdenum are cereal grains, liver, kidney, peas, and beans. Promotes normal growth and healthy teeth and gums. Possible results of molybdenum deficiencies are unknown. Deficiencies of copper may involve molybdenum.

POTASSIUM

Natural sources of potassium are sardines, lentils, molasses, potatoes, parsnips, nuts, and whole-grain cereals. Sodium and potassium work together to maintain water balance in body tissue and cells. Promotes regular heartbeat. Works in maintaining the transfer of nutrients to the cells. Potassium deficiencies may result in: weakness, dehydration, slow growth, and irregular or rapid heartbeat.

SELENIUM

Natural sources of selenium are liver, milk, tuna, egg yolks, mushrooms, wheat germ, bran, whole grain cereals, chicken, and garlic. Works with vitamin E as an antioxidant. Promotes healthy muscles. An essential element for healthy skin and coat. Selenium deficiencies may result in: weight loss, poor skin and coat condition, and tooth decay.

SODIUM

The main source of sodium is table salt. Other sources include, ham, bacon, canned sardines, and snack foods. Pets usually receive an adequate amount of salt through their diet and therefore adding salt is seldom necessary. Sodium regulates the fluid balance in the body. It is extremely important in maintaining blood pressure. Sodium deficiencies may result in: muscle cramps, fatigue, hair loss, dry skin, and slow growth.

ZINC

Natural sources of zinc are whole grain products, egg yolks, molasses, wheat germ, garlic, fish, turkey, and lamb. Zinc is an antioxidant. Promotes healing of wounds, and normal growth development. Zinc deficiencies may result in: slow wound healing, decreased growth, poor appetite, and prostate problems in older dogs.

HELPFUL HINTS

FLEAS

A natural diet is one of the best defenses for your pets against fleas. Fleas have been one of the major complaints of pet owners over the years. Brewer's yeast, added to the diet, was for many years touted as a sure cure for this pesky problem. Recently, information has come to light suggesting that the large amount of brewer's yeast necessary to eliminate fleas might cause health problems for your pet. Instead of adding brewer's yeast to the diet, try sprinkling it on your pet. Thoroughly rub it into the coat to make sure it reaches the skin. Fleas cannot stand the smell of yeast and will jump off your pet (and you too). When sprinkling the brewer's yeast, make sure you take the dog or cat outdoors; otherwise you will have additional fleas in your home. Combing your pet with a very fine tooth comb will also eliminate fleas and flea eggs. Again, make sure that you do this outdoors, and keep a container of water (rubbing alcohol is even better) handy to drown the fleas as you take them out of the comb.

Although I have never encountered a flea problem in the house, many people mention a "sure cure." Sprinkle ordinary table salt on carpets, floors, furniture, and especially in cracks and crevices around baseboards where fleas hide. Wait one or two hours and vacuum. Salt will kill the fleas and the flea eggs. Wash any bedding your pet sleeps on. However, about the only way to really rid fleas from the house is vacuum, vacuum, vacuum.

Raw garlic fed to pets has also been used as a preventative measure. The chemical, allicin, found in garlic can cause stomach problems when fed in large amounts, so feed raw garlic with care. Cooked garlic or garlic in a freeze-dried form, kyloic, will not cause stomach upset and works just as well as raw garlic. I grow garlic for my cats and also cut up some of the green in their food. Plant individual garlic bulbs in your garden or in pots in the house. Place in a sunny window, water, and in a few weeks the garlic grows tall, grass-like greens. The garlic grass is not as strong as the cloves, but it is just as potent. The cats love to nibble on it.

Never put a commercial flea collar on your pet. These can cause severe allergies, and I have seen cats where their necks become raw after having a flea collar on for only a few days. These collars contain nerve gases that can enter the blood stream and cause a myriad of problems, including death.

Carbaryl, an insecticide found in flea collars is considered "moderately hazardous" according to the World Health Organization (WHO). Catherine O'Driscoll, *Canine Health Census*, writes that Carbaryl "is a mutagen, and it is carcinogenic and teratogenic in laboratory animals [it can cause mutation in cells]. It can induce cancer, and it can cause birth defects in lab animals when absorbed in pregnancy. Carbaryl is reported to be more toxic to dogs than to other animals."[9] When we put one of these collars on our pets, they are breathing these toxic substances twenty-four hours a day. A flea collar on a large or long-hair dog is ineffective. They may kill a few fleas around the neck, but hundreds of fleas are still reproducing in the carpets, furniture, and bedding.[10]

Flea powders, sprays, shampoos, dips, and even pills are available to rid your pet of fleas, but how safe are these substances? Read the warnings on the label. However, these warnings are designed to protect you, not your pet. "Wash hands immediately after applying." "Don't breathe the dust." "Don't apply to a pet if a fish tank is near." If the chemicals in these products can kill fish, what are these chemicals doing to your cats and dogs? They breathe in the dust, and the first thing a cat does if something is applied to her coat, is to lick it off.

There are many horror stories regarding cats and small dogs and the application of these powders, shampoos, and dips: drooling, seizures, paralysis, and death. In 1984 before I became aware of the problems associated with these substances, I used a flea powder on my cats. The product contained Rotenone and Dichlorophene. The first time I dusted the cats, I used very little as they seemed distressed at having something rubbed into their coats. One week later, and as per instructions, I reapplied the product. All the cats began to salivate, and within twenty-four hours my lynx-point Siamese, Whisper, was very ill. Whisper died two weeks later of renal failure. My other cats did survive, but that was the last time that I ever used any commercial flea preparation on any of my pets.

An excellent spray, which can be applied to either dogs or cats and which is nontoxic, consists of lemons and water. Cut three lemons in quarters, cover with water, bring to a boil and simmer for fifteen minutes. Let cool, then spray or rub it into the fur. Again, as with garlic or brewer's yeast, the smell deters the fleas. This also soothes irritated skin.

Hot Spots

A skin irritation that usually starts with flea bites and causes raw red spots is considered a "hot spot." Dogs or cats will chew at the spot until it actually becomes infected. One safe and nontoxic treatment is bathing the area with vitamin C mixed in a glass of cool water or bathing the area with cold tea. Both have astringent properties. Or open a capsule of vitamin E and apply the liquid generously to the affected area. Follow this procedure two or three times per day. Try to keep your pet from licking it off before it has a chance to sink into the area. These remedies will not work overnight, but they are safe and effective.

Toxic Plants

Cats are far worse for nibbling on plants than dogs. My cats would walk across the ceiling to get at a plant. The list is lengthy of plants that can make your pet ill or even kill them. Among them are lily of the valley, bulbs, (tulip, hyacinth, narcissus, daffodil, crocus), needle-point ivy, mistletoe, foxglove, castor bean, philodendron, tomato, and rhubarb plants. Because it is such an extensive list it would be wise to check with your garden center before purchasing a plant for your home or garden. Try growing some plants just for your pets. Catnip, wheat grass, many sprouts, even grass you plant in your garden, all can be grown in the house, and will provide vitamins and minerals for your pet.

LAWN SPRAYS

While we are on the topic of toxic substances, a herbicide, 2,4-Dichlorophenoxyacetic Acid (2,4-D), which is used by home owners and lawn care companies, has been linked to canine malignant lymphoma. This study was undertaken by the National Cancer Institute. The report states,"the risk of canine lymphoma rose to a twofold excess with four or more yearly applications of 2,4-D. This herbicide has also been implicated as the source of non-Hodgkins disease in humans."[11]

One of the many herbicides that contain deadly dioxins is 2,4-D. It is used not only by home owners for weed control in their lawns but also by farmers as it is cheaper and more effective than other weed-killers. Doctors urge people using this herbicide to wear masks, boots, and gloves for protection.[12] Cats walk over grass sprayed with this chemical. They then lick their paws thus ingesting this toxic substance. Dogs walk and roll in grass sprayed with 2,4-D and if they have even a small cut, 2,4-D can get into the system. This herbicide is found in more than 1,500 over-the-counter weed-killers. Our health, the health of our pets and the environment are at risk when we apply these chemicals. Is it worth it? Is it worth having the perfect weed-free lawn?

FEEDING A SICK PET

Many years ago, when one of my cats had an upper respiratory infection, I became desperate. The veterinarian advised that we had to get food into him, but because the cats nose was very stuffy, he could not smell the food and therefore would not eat. At that point in time, I was still feeding my pets commercial pet food. We purchased every brand of food available in the hope that he would eat, but nothing worked. Finally, I purchased a bottle of all-meat baby food (beef). I put a small amount on his nose, and he immediately licked it off. I continued this three or four times, and gradually he began to lick it off my finger. Once the cat began to eat, he recovered very quickly.

Over the years, I have advised many people to try all-meat baby food if their pet is not eating, and it seems to have worked for all who have tried it. Beef, chicken, or turkey are the baby foods of choice, avoid lamb. According to a recent article in *Petfood Industry* magazine, "Many human baby food lamb recipes contain onion powder, an ingredient that may trigger a form of anemia called 'Heinz-body anemia'."[13] It is also to be noted that some lamb based cat foods also contain onion powder. Read labels.

Any strong-smelling food, such as fish, liver, cheese, can usually entice a pet to start eating. As with children, pets have a tendency to dehydrate quickly, and a sick pet usually does not want to drink. Before you try forcing fluids on your cat or dog, try giving him tomato juice, clam and tomato juice, evaporated milk, broth or watered-down baby food. When all else fails, fill a syringe or eye dropper with fluid, place in the side of the mouth and slowly squeeze the liquid into the mouth. Do it slowly and with a break so that the pet does not choke.

PILLS

Giving pills to pets can be a real challenge. I've watched our veterinarian and he makes it seem so easy. Easy, that is, until you get home and it's pill time. If one of my cats or dogs had to have a pill, I had to devise ways of getting it into my pet without the battle of having to force it down the cat or dog's throat.

Dogs are easy. Wrap the pill in a piece of meat or strong-smelling cheese, or make a peanut butter sandwich with the pill in the middle. I always give them a few pieces of the meat, cheese, or sandwich without the pill before I give them the one containing the pill. If you give them another piece of food immediately after the one with the pill, they are in such a rush to get it that they swallow the pill immediately.

Cats are a different story. Often crushing the pill into a fine powder and mixing it with either salmon or tuna works well. If this fails, crush the pill and mix it with baby food. Beef is the best as it has a stronger flavor. Put a little of the plain baby food on their nose, and let them lick it off. Then put the baby food containing the crushed-up pill on their nose. They can't stand to have anything on their noses so they will lick it off. If this fails, crush the pill, mix it with watered-down baby food, place in a syringe and slowly squeeze it into their mouth.

BATH TIME

Your cat or small dog needs a bath, but they hate this procedure. When I acquired a kitten covered in fleas, bathing was the only quick elimination of these insects. Although small, Felix could put up a real fight when there was water involved. As I have never, (and never will) declawed my cats, I knew that giving Felix a bath would result in scratches on my hands and arms. Solution: I used a pillow case. I put Felix in the pillow case up to her neck and tied it loosely. She fought, but I escaped scratches. There are other benefits to the pillow case: shampoo can be rubbed through the pillow case, and rinsing is easy.

ARTHRITIS

Two of my dogs developed arthritis in their hips when they were senior citizens. They had difficulty getting up, especially in the morning. Although they had warm beds, winters in Canada are very cold. I felt that if they were warmer, as with humans, they might be able to move more freely in the morning. Solution: I used heating pads that I put in their beds, on a low temperature, under a light blanket. Within one day, the improvement was very noticeable. Do not put a heating pad in a bed if the dog or cat is incontinent. A hot water bottle can also be used although it does cool off during the night.

RAWHIDE BONES

Numerous cases of deaths in dogs have been reported in the last five or six years due to rawhide bones. Pieces become lodged in their throats and the dogs have choked to death. Try giving your dog a knuckle bone or a marrow bone. Don't leave the animal alone with the bones, as he or she may be able to chew pieces off. Dogs also seem to lick the nylon bones. If you can get small marrow bones, cats enjoy these very much and they are excellent for keeping teeth clean.

People have different opinions about the wisdom of letting your dog chew on bones. Some veterinarians state that this will wear their teeth down and even break them off. Other veterinarians are of the opposite opinion, stating that bones help keep a dog's teeth clean. Regardless of your belief, never give turkey, chicken, or other small bones to dogs or cats because pieces can break off and become lodged in their throat or intestines.

To many of us, our pets are a part of our family. Give your pet a healthy diet, a warm place to sleep, exercise, and love. In return, he or she will provide you with years of enjoyment, friendship, and unconditional love.

Photo: Sumner Fowler

Chapter Eight

Resources for Consumer Action

An article in the *Petfood Industry* magazine in 1996 stated that a single cat, living fifteen years, ingesting three and one half pounds of food per week, is worth $2,000 (U.S.) in sales to the company who "secures its loyalty." The figure for a medium-size dog, living fifteen years can garner $3,500 (U.S.) for the company that can secure the pet's loyalty to its product.[1]

As consumers we have the right, the obligation, to know what we are getting for our loyalty, and most importantly, exactly what is in the food we are feeding our pets. Their health and welfare lie in our hands, yet the commercial pet food industry provides us with such vague terms we really do not know what we are actually feeding them.

Changes must be made in the labeling of these foods. Changes must be made in the ingredients used. And consumers need to have a clear understanding of the nutritional value and digestibility of these products.

The first mode of action is to contact the manufacturer of the pet food you purchase. State your complaints, advise the representative that you want answers, changes, and above all the full truth of ingredients used. If the company cannot and will not accept changes in their policies, go elsewhere. When pet food manufacturers realize that consumer dollars will no longer support their product, it is possible they will consider change. If no other company is found that can provide an acceptable diet for your pet, cook for your pet.

Do not address your complaints or concerns to the company in general. You will get the standard pat answers that tell you nothing. Write to the president, chairperson, and CEO of the company. If their response is not acceptable, restate your concerns and expectations and try again.

Be specific when you contact pet food companies about your concerns. Request that the particular pet food company:

(1) Define ingredients, meat meal, tankage, digest, by-products, and other vague terms.

(2) Provide data on safety studies of additives, ingredients, processing, and field trial studies.

(3) Change the label so that the "nutritional value" panel realistically supplies details on the food's nutritional value.

(4) Use healthy ingredients.

(5) List on the label whether their formulation is variable or fixed.[2]

* * *

The list below provides the names and addresses of the president/CEOs of four of the largest pet food companies. Included is a list of some of their products. As most of the pet foods sold in Canada are produced by the multinationals in the United States, I suggest that rather than addressing their concerns to the Canadian affiliate, send them directly to the head office in the United States.

Remember, pet food companies also produce an extensive line of private label foods and prescription diets. Check the label of the food you are using for the name of the company. Most companies list an 800 number on the label. Call the given number, ask for the name of the president/CEO, and address all requests and questions to him/her, no one else.

RALSTON PURINA
William P. Stiritz
Chairman, President, and CEO
Ralston Purina
Checkerboard Square
St. Louis, MO 63164

Dog Foods: Dog Chow, Puppy Chow, O.N.E., Kibbles & Chunks, Fit & Trim, Gravy, Main Stay, Chuck Wagon, Stampede, Pro Plan, Field

Master, Lucky Dog, Hi-Pro, Prime, Butchers, Moist & Chunky.

Cat Foods: Purina Premium, Unique, Cat Chow, Meow Mix, Alley Cat, Kitten Chow, O.N.E., Cat Menu.

NESTLE
Joe Weller
President and CEO
Nestle USA, Inc
800 N. Brand Blvd.
Glendale, CA 91203

Dog Foods: Come 'N Get It, Alpo, Friskies, Jim Dandy, Classic Dinner, Hunters Choice, Alpo Senior, Mighty Dog, Friskies Gourmet, Blue Mountain.

Cat Foods: Friskies Buffet, Fancy Feast, Alpo Cat Food, Friskies Kitten, Fresh Catch, Bright Eyes, Chef's Blend, Fish Ahoy.

MARS (AKA EFFEM FOODS)
Forrest E. Mars, Jr.
Chairman, CEO, and Co-President
Mars
6885 Elm St.
McLean, VA 22101-3810

Dog Foods: Meal Time, Kal Kan, Pedigree, Pedigree Choice Cuts, Pedigree Select Dinners, Pedigree Puppy.

Cat Foods: Whiskas, Sheba, Whiskas Expert, Crave Whiskas.

HEINZ
Anthony J.F. O'Reilly
Chairman, President, and CEO
Heinz
600 Grant St.
Pittsburg PA 15219

Dog Foods: Gravy Train, Dry Cycle, Hearty Chunks, Choice Blend, Tuffy, Skippy, Cycle, Ken-L-Ration, Reward, King Kuts, Vets, Kibbles 'N Bits, Tender Chops, Dinner Rounds, Love Me Tender Chunks, Gaines Burgers.

Cat Foods: 9-Lives, Amore, Kozy Kitten, Puss 'n Boots, Pounce.

In 1995 Heinz purchased the pet food division of Quaker Oats. Other acquisitions: Earth Elements Inc., California, marketed under the brand of Nature's Recipe Pet Foods. In 1996, H.J. Heinz Company of Canada Ltd., acquired the pet food division of Martin Feed Mill Limited of Elmira, Ontario, Canada.[3]

Most likely you will receive a lengthy, evasive reply that feels like a pat on the head. Don't be deterred. Write again, making it clear that you want the issues addressed. Keep writing until you are satisfied. If you are lucky, you may receive a second reply, most likely still evasive, and you will hear no more. "Ignore them and they'll go away," seems the typical mode of industry and government. Next step, go to the government agency responsible for the industry.

IN THE UNITED STATES:
Pet Food Institute
1200 19th St. NW
Suite 300
Washington, DC 20036-2401

IN CANADA:
Pet Food Association of Canada
1435 Goldthorpe Road
Mississauga, Ontario
L5G 3R2

The Pet Food Institute is a pet food association representing the interests of the industry in the United States. The Pet Food Association of Canada, a voluntary organization, also represents the manufacturers and has developed a Nutrition Assurance Program (NAP), which it states is to "establish consumer confidence through consistent claims of nutritional adequacy." They have also adopted the nutritional levels required for dog and cat foods as determined by the Association of American Feed Control Officials (AAFCO). However, neither the Pet Food Institute nor the Pet Food Association have any input as to the ingredients used in the foods.

The AAFCO is composed of federal and state officials that regulate label text and ingredient definitions. Label text is much too generalized. The AAFCO stamp on pet food labels indicates that the particular food meets its standards. "However, according to the Animal Protection

Institute of America: Investigative Report on Pet Food, AAFCO standards have been challenged as lacking scientific variability due to the wide variance in ingredients and the apparent arbitrariness of how minimum nutrient requirements were established."[5]

At a 1996 meeting of the AAFCO's Pet Food Committee (PFC), the chair of the PFC, Rod Noel, DVM, was asked to "share his thoughts on pet food regulations." Among other things, he noted, "There needs to be a certain amount of uniformity in labeling which allows the consumer to understand and compare labels among products and companies. There needs to be some assurance that the consumer is getting the nutrition required to properly sustain their pet's healthy life."[6]

Pet food manufacturers established themselves as an industry about thirty to forty years and now they realize that the consumer needs this assurance. Perhaps consumers are now asking questions, becoming concerned about the ills befalling their pets, and finally, realizing that there may be a link to the foods they are feeding and the myriad of diseases their pets are experiencing. Is the pet food industry going to provide us with these assurances? Is the FDA/CVM or the AAFCO going to assure us that what we are feeding our pet on a daily basis is not having detrimental effects?

Dr. Noel added, "A major concern is truthfulness in labeling. This covers all nutritional claims or other types of claims made on product labels."[7] As chair of the AAFCO, Dr. Noel must be cognizant that consumers are questioning, at great length, the contents of these cans and bags of pet food they are feeding their companion animals.

If your state has adopted the AAFCO regulations, you may be able to use the AAFCO as a starting point to initiate changes. To ascertain if your state has adopted AAFCO regulations, contact your state department of agriculture. Be sure to specifically mention pet food as some states have regulations for livestock feed only. AAFCO regulations do not apply in Canada, although they do have a representative with the Ministry of Agriculture and Agri-Food in Ottawa.

Tim Phillips, DVM, editor of *Petfood Industry*, wrote an article entitled "Scandal Hungry?" This article was written because of an investigation of the pet food industry by two magazine shows, "Dateline" and "20/20." I had spoken to one of the reporters, Diane Persky, at great length, and she seemed extremely knowledgeable about what was happening with regard to the rendering of pets and the ingredients used in pet food. In his editorial, Dr. Phillips writes, "The use of scare-mongering language to hype a story is not uncommon. Sensationalistic language may boost ratings, but also scares and misinforms consumers."[8]

According to the article, Jim Corbin, DVM, who provides information to the Pet Food Institute, and is affiliated with the University of Illinois, was also contacted by a television news magazine show (not identified in the article). In Corbin's follow-up letter to the reporter (also unidentified) he writes, in part, "More is known about the nutritional requirements of dogs and cats than is known about the nutritional requirements of humans."[9] He also went on to write, "Pet food packaging depicts package contents much more accurately than does packaging for human food."[10]

After noting Dr. Corbin's comments, Dr. Phillips continues in the article, "Let's hope Dr. Corbin's efforts to put things in perspective paid off."[11] Dr. Phillips then suggested, "Positive action," which the industry can take if contacted by one of these investigative reporters. "Still, we must contend with consumers' perception of reality—no matter how unscientific that may be. Blame-fixing and denial are not effective approaches in discussing risk," writes Phillips. "Taking positive action is." He then lists some suggestions as to how proceed if the company is contacted by the media: "Make certain the proper company spokesperson handles the call. Be a good listener. A person's perception of risk often is colored by his/her perspective, which may be radically different from your own. Avoid raw technical data."[12]

As of mid-1997, neither of these television shows has aired a program specifically on the pet food industry. In late 1996, one show in Texas, "eye tv," did air a series on what could actually be the ingredients in pet food. Two days later, I received an email from the producer in Austin, Texas: "On Thursday night we had three veterinarians answering phone calls in the newsroom," she wrote. "The phones rang for two and a half hours. The series barely scratched the surface—I couldn't possibly have imagined this kind of outpouring."[13]

The pet food industry holds a convention every year in Chicago. This event is usually held at the Hyatt Regency O'Hare for two days in April. It brings together speakers from the U.S. government, the industry, and academia. Some of the topics covered at their 1996 convention included: reducing fecal output, canned pet food: problem solving, and pet allergies: myth or fact. The cost to attend this two-day forum, depending on the time of registration is $570 to $670 (U.S.), which makes it rather costly for a concerned consumer to attend.[14]

People are concerned. And consumers have a right to know. It is up to us to pressure the pet food industry, AAFCO, and any government body that might have input, to regulate this industry.

In the United States, the arm of the government that supposedly oversees the labeling of pet food is the FDA/CVM. Its main concern is claims made by companies as it relates to the health of the pet such as the prevention of FUS (Feline Urological Syndrome).

In Canada, the Federal Ministry of Agriculture oversees ingredients used in livestock feed. There are no federal or provincial regulations as to the ingredients used in commercial pet food.

Another method which may be attempted, a method which I refer to as the "back door" approach, is the advertisements on labels, in magazines, and on television. These advertisements depict quality meats, grains, and fats. According to my research over the past seven years, this is not what we are getting in pet food. Which leads me to ask, "Can these advertisements be categorized as false and misleading advertising?"

If you want to investigate this further, or lodge a complaint as a concerned citizen, you can contact the government agency that handles investigations into false and misleading advertising:

IN THE UNITED STATES
Federal Trade Commission
Advertising Practices
6th Street and Pennsylvania Ave. NW
Washington, DC 20580

IN CANADA:
Industry Canada
Consumer Products Directorate
Place du Portage
50 Victoria Street, 16th Floor
Hull, Quebec
K1A OC9

One person, on his or her own, is not going to make drastic changes. The industry and government will listen—but little, if anything, will be done. There is strength in numbers. If enough pressure is put on these government agencies, and on the pet food manufacturers, they may start to listen. Form a group, and join other pet companion advocates. Write letters to state and federal representatives or members of parliament in Canada. These people want to be re-elected and will listen to the concerns of their constituents. Circulate petitions and send them to your representatives. Submit a citizen's petition on behalf of your group to the FDA/CVM, requesting a ban on the use of diseased, condemned, or contaminated material in commercial pet food.

IN THE UNITED STATES:
FDA
Director, Center for Veterinary Medicine
HF-1, 5600 Fishers Lane
Rockville, MD 20857

IN CANADA:
Minister of Agriculture
Ottawa, Ontario
Canada K1A OC5

It is frustrating, but don't give up as it is only we, the pet owners, who can initiate change. One small step is better than sitting back and doing nothing. Historically, groups boycotting a particular food—taking their consumer dollars elsewhere—has worked wonders.

I have listed some of the groups that have fought numerous battles, in many avenues, for companion animals. They no doubt would welcome someone to work in the area of pet food investigation and organization.

In the United States many groups exist in every state. The following list includes a few of the larger organizations that you might consider working with.

ANIMAL PROTECTION INSTITUTE OF AMERICA
2831 Fruitridge Road
Sacramento, CA 95820

PEOPLE FOR THE ETHICAL TREATMENT OF ANIMALS (PETA)
PO Box 42516
Washington, DC 20015

ACTION FOR ANIMALS NETWORK
PO Box 9039
Alexandria, VA 22304

AMERICAN SOCIETY FOR THE PREVENTION OF CRUELTY TO ANIMALS
424 E. 92nd Street
New York, NY 10128

EARTHHEART FOUNDATION
106 N. Wisconsin St.
DePere, WI 54115

NORTH CAROLINA NETWORK FOR ANIMALS
PO Box 33565
Raleigh, NC 27636

IN CANADA:

ANIMAL ALLIANCE OF CANADA
221 Broadview Ave.
Suite 101
Toronto, Ontario
M4M 2G3

THE KINDNESS CLUB
65 Brunswick St.
Fredericton, NB
E3B 1G5

VANCOUVER HUMANE SOCIETY
PO Box 18119
2225 West 41st Avenue
Vancouver, BC
V6M 4L3

Change takes time and effort. If we are going to continue to feed commercial food to our companion pets, there must be change. Only through the efforts of consumers will these changes come about. Our animal companions deserve it.

SELECT BIBLIOGRAPHY

Belfield, Wendell O., and Zucker, Martin, *How to Have a Healthier Dog*, New York: Doubleday and Company, 1981.

Billinghurst, Ian, *Give Your Dog a Bone*, Australia: Bridge Printers, 1993.

Cooke, David C., *Euthanasia of the Companion Animal: Animal Disposal: Fact or Fiction*, Philadelphia, Pennsylvania: Charles Press, 1988.

Fox, Michael W., *Eating with Conscience: The Bioethics of Food*, Troutdale, Oregon: NewSage Press, 1997.

Franco, Don A., *The Genus Salmonella*. Alexandria, Virginia: National Renderers Association, Alexandria, Virginia, 1985.

Frazier, Anitra with Norma Eckroate, *The New Natural Cat*, New York: Penguin, 1990.

Griffith, H. Winter, *Complete Guide to Vitamins, Minerals and Supplements*. Tuscon, Arizona: Fisher Books, 1988.

Lazarus, Pat, *Keep Your Pet Healthy the Natural Way*, New Canaan, Connecticut: Keats Publishing, 1986.

Mindell, Earl, *Earl Mindell's Vitamin Bible*, New York: Warner Books, 1979.

O'Driscoll, Catherine, *Who Killed the Darling Buds of May: Vaccines*, Longnor, England: Abbywood Publishing, 1997.

Pitcairn, Richard H., and Susan Hubble Pitcairn. *Dr. Pitcairn's Complete Guide to Natural Health for Dogs and Cats*, Emmaus: Rodale, 1995.

Plechner, Alfred J., and Zucker, Martin, *Pet Allergies: Remedies for an Epidemic*, Inglewood: Wilshire Book Company, 1986.

Sundlof, S.F., *Antimicrobial Drug Residues in Food Producing Animals: Therapy in Veterinary Medicine*, Ames, Iowa: Iowa State University Press, 1993.

Wysong, R.L., *Rationale for Animal Nutrition*, Midland, Michigan: Inquiry Press, 1993.

ENDNOTES

Chapter One: The Case Against Commercial Pet Food

1. Personal correspondence with Joan MacLean, pet food company representative, February 27, 1990.

2. Hope Laboratories, Report, March 13, 1990.

3. Ministry of Agriculture and Food, Veterinary Laboratory Services Branch, Report, Guelph, Ontario, June 6, 1990.

4. Mann Testing Laboratories, Report, Mississauga, Ontario, July 3, 1990.

5. Personal correspondence with Cecil F. Brownie, DVM, PhD, DABVT, DABT, toxicologist, North Carolina State University College of Veterinary Medicine, Raleigh, North Carolina, October 22, 1990.

6. Personal correspondence with: Barry Blakley, DVM, PhD., University of Saskatchewan, September 13, 1990; Larry J. Thompson, DVM, Cornell University, September 18, 1990; James D. Ferguson, VMD, University of Pennsylvania, October 5, 1990; Michael W. Knight, DVM, University of Illinois at Urbana-Champaign, October 12, 1990; Robert Poppenga, DVM, PhD, Michigan State University, October 16, 1990; Dr. Michael Mount, DVM, PhD, University of California, Davis, January 3, 1991.

7. Personal correspondence with Robert Puls, PAg toxicologist, Ministry of Agriculture and Fisheries, Abbotsford, British Columbia, November 4, 1991.

8. Personal correspondence with R.W. Wilson, DVM, Veterinary Laboratory Services, Guelph, Ontario, December 5, 1990.

9. Final Report. Veterinary Laboratory Services, Guelph, Ontario, January 16, 1991.

10. Ontario Court (General Division), "Claim," June 4, 1991.

11. Provincial Court (Civil Division), "Defence," June 28, 1991.

12. Personal correspondence, Douglas E. Grundy, Toronto, Ontario, January 10, 1992.

13. The Honorable Judge S. Lerner, Provincial Court (Civil Division), "Summation", January 14, 1992.

14. Ontario Court (General Division), "Motion," January 28, 1992.

15. Ontario Court (General Division), "Reasons for Judgement," April 1, 1993.

16. Ontario Court (General Division), "Defendant's Submissions as to Costs," April 21, 1993.

Chapter Two: Companion Animals in Pet Food

1. John Eckhouse, "How Your Dogs and Cats Get Recycled Into Pet Food," *San Francisco Chronicle*, February 19, 1990.

2. Personal correspondence with the Ministry of Agriculture and Food, London, Ontario, July 10, 1992.

3. Personal correspondence with the Ministry of Agriculture and Food, Peterborough, Ontario, June 5, 1992.

4. Personal correspondence with Alex Couture, Inc., Quebec, July 15, 1992.

5. Personal correspondence with Gouvernement du Quebec, August 14, 1992.

6. Sandra Blakeslee, "Disease Fear Prompts New Look at Rendering," *New York Times*, March 11, 1997.

7. Personal correspondence with Laurenco, Ville Ste-Catherine, Quebec, July 18, 1994.

8. Personal correspondence with USDA, Food Safety and Inspection Service, Washington, D.C., June 24, 1994.

9. Ibid., July 29, 1994.

10. Personal correspondence with Department of Health and Human Services, FDA, Rockville Maryland, July 12, 1994.

11. 1993 Report of the American Veterinary Medical Association Panel on Euthanasia. *Journal of the American Veterinary Medical Association*, Vol. 202, No. 2, January 15, 1993, pp. 238, 239.

12. John J. O'Connor, DVM, MPH; Clarence M. Stowe, VMD, PhD; Robert R. Robinson, BVSc, MPH, PhD, "Fate of Sodium Pentobarbital in Rendered Material." *Am J Vet Res*, Vol. 46, No. 8, August 1995, pp. 1721, 1723.

13. North American Compendium, "T-61 Euthanasia Solution," *Compendium of Veterinary Products*, Compendium Code No. 1750950, 1996.

14. Personal correspondence with the Department of Natural Resources, Palmer, Alaska, January 12, 1995.

15. Personal correspondence with the Department of Agriculture and Industries, Montgomery, Alabama, January 6, 1995.

16. Personal correspondence with the Arizona Department of Agriculture, Phoenix, Arizona, January 9, 1995.

17. Personal correspondence with the Florida Department of Agriculture and Consumer Services, January 5, 1995.

18. Personal correspondence with the Department of Agriculture, Atlanta, Georgia, January 9, 1995.

19. Personal correspondence with the Department of Agriculture, Boise, Idaho, January 5, 1995.

20. Personal correspondence with the Department of Agriculture, Springfield, Illinois, January 4, 1995.

21. Personal correspondence with the Indiana State Chemist and Seed Commissioner, West Lafayette, Indiana, January 1, 1995.

22. Personal correspondence with the University of Kentucky, College of Agriculture, Lexington, Kentucky, April 7, 1995.

23. Personal correspondence with the Department of Food and Agriculture, Boston, Massachusetts, January 31, 1995.

24. Personal correspondence with the Department of Agriculture, Jefferson City, Missouri, January 25, 1995.

25. Personal correspondence with the Department of Agriculture, New Jersey, January 10, 1995.

26. Personal correspondence with the Department of Agriculture and Markets, Albany, New York, January 11, 1995.

27. Personal correspondence with the Department of Agriculture, Raleigh, North Carolina, January 10, 1995.

28. Personal correspondence with the Department of Agriculture, Columbus, Ohio, February 1, 1995.

29. Personal correspondence with the Department of Agriculture, Oklahoma City, Oklahoma, January 19, 1995.

30. Personal correspondence with the Department of Agriculture, Salem, Oregon, January 9, 1995.

31. Personal correspondence with the Department of Environmental Management, Providence, Rhode Island, January 18, 1995.

32. Personal correspondence with the Department of Agriculture, Columbia, South Carolina, January 18, 1995.

33. Personal correspondence with the Department of Agriculture, Cheyenne, Wyoming, January 18, 1995.

34. Personal correspondence with the Department of Health Services, Sacramento, California, February 6, 1996.

35. Personal correspondence with the Gouvernement du Quebec, Quebec, August 14, 1992.

36. Van Smith, "Meltdown," *City Paper,* Baltimore, Maryland, September 27, 1995.

Chapter Three: Mad Cow Disease and How It Relates to Our Pets

1. Michael Greger, "The Public Health Implications of Mad Cow Disease," Vegetarian Summerfest '96: A World Vegetarian Congress, August 1, 1996, citing "Ministers Hostile to Advise on BSE," *New Scientist,* March 30, 1996, p. 4.

2. Ibid., citing Paul Brown, Rebecca Smithers, and Sarah Bosely, "Beef Warning Sparks Panic," *Guardian,* March 2, 1996, p. 1.

3. Ibid., citing D.M. Taylor, "Bovine Spongiform Encephalophy," *Medical Laboratory Science,* 1992, pp. 334-9.

4. Ibid., citing Pat Phillips, "Skepticism about Prions Wanes a Bit," *Medical World News,* December 1991, p. 21.

5. Physicians Committee for Responsible Medicine, "Mad Cow Disease: The Risk to the U.S." Paper, Washington, D.C., Summer 1996, p. 4.

6. Greger, *op. cit.,* citing Joel Bleifuss, "How Now Mad Cow," *In These Times,* January 24, 1994, pp. 12, 13.

7. Ibid., citing William Hueston, Anita M. Bleem, and Kevin D. Walker, "Bovine Spongiform Encephalopathy," *Animal Health Insight,* Fall 1992, pp. 1-7.

8. "Mad Elk Disease Feared," *London Free Press,* London, Ontario, April 28, 1996.

9. Greger, *op. cit.,* citing R.F. Marsh and R.A. Bessen, "Epidemiologic and Experimental Studies on Transmissible Mink Encephalopathy," *Developments in Biological Standardization,* 80, 1993, pp. 111-118.

10. Ibid., citing United States Department of Agriculture: Animal and Plant Health Inspection Service, "Bovine Spongiform Encephalopathy: Implications for the United States," Fort Collins: Centers for Epidemiology and Animal Health, 1993.

11. Ibid., citing Joel McNair, "BSE: A Ticking Time Bomb in Downer Cows?" *Agri-View,* 17, June 1993.

12. Statement by anonymous United States Department of Agriculture employee, January 11, 1997.

13. Physicians Committee, *op. cit.,* p. 4.

14. Greger, *op. cit.* citing United States Department of Agriculture: Animal and Plant Health Inspection Service, "Bovine Spongiform Encephalopathy," Fact Sheet, Fort Collins, Colorado: USDA, March 1996.

15. Physicians Committee, *op. cit.,* p. 4.

16. Food and Drug Administration, Federal Register of August 29, 1994 (59FR44584), Vol. 61, No. 94, Washington, D.C.: Department of Health and Human Services, 1994.

17. Personal correspondence with Dr. Eric Haapapuro, Physicians Committee for Responsible Medicine, July 15, 1996.

18. Personal Correspondence with Agriculture Canada, Ottawa, July 4, 1996.

19. "Mad Cow and Oprah," edited transcript of the April 16, 1996 "Oprah Winfrey Show," *Earth Island Journal,* Summer 1996, p. 34.

20. Ibid.

21. *Pure Food Campaign,* Organization newsletter, August 24, 1995.

22. Ibid.

23. Personal correspondence with David Dzanis, DVM, Center for Veterinary Medicine, Rockville, Maryland, May 5, 1996.

24. Mark M. Robinson, "Bovine Spongiform Encephalopathy Only a British Concern?" Proceedings of the American Association of Bovine Practitioners Annual Convention. January 1992, p. 19.

25. Joel Bleifuss, "Killer Beef," *In These Times,* May 31, 1993, pp. 12-15.

26. Mark Caldwell, "Mad Cows and Wild Proteins," *Discover,* April 1991, pp. 69-74; and Daniel Pearl, "British Suppressed Beef Disease Facts for Years," *Wall Street Journal,* March 22, 1996.

27. Physicians Committee, *op. cit.,* p. 2.

28. Ibid.

29. Personal correspondence with Richard Pitcairn, DVM, Eugene, Oregon, August 5, 1996.

30. Ibid.

31. Personal correspondence with Scott McEwen, DVM, Guelph, Ontario, October 21, 1996.

32. Personal correspondence with Andrew Mackin, DVM, Royal School of Veterinary Medicine, Edinburgh, Scotland, October 28, 1996.

33. Associated Press, April 22, 1997.

34. Roger Highfield, *Daily Telegraph,* April 29, 1997.

35. "Bovine Spongiform Encephalopathy Statement," *Petfood Industry,* May/June 1996.

36. Jim Corbin, "Pet Foods and Feeding," *Feedstuffs,* July 17, 1996, p. 84.

37. Michael Greger, "The Public Health Implications of Mad Cow Disease," Vegetarian Summerfest '96: A World Vegetarian Congress, August 1, 1996.

38. Physicians Committee, *op. cit.,* p. 2.

39. John Stauber and Sheldon Rampton, "The US 'Mad Cow' Cover-Up," *Earth Island Journal,* Summer 1996, p. 29.

Chapter Four: Sources of Meat, Carbohydrates, and Fiber

1. Personal correspondence with the Ministry of Agriculture, Ottawa, Ontario, April 4, 1994.

2. David C. Cooke, "Euthanasia of the Companion Animal," " Animal Disposal: Fact or Fiction," Amercian Veterinarian Medical Association, Panel on Euthanasia, 1988, p. 227.

3. Tim Phillips, "Rendered Products Guide," *Petfood Industry,* January/February 1994, pp. 12-17.

4. Meat Inspection Act (Ontario), Ontario Regulation 632/92, 1992.

5. Association of American Feed Control Officials,

Official Publication, 1994.

6. Personal correspondence with the Department of Agriculture, State of Delaware, September 23, 1994.

7. Personal correspondence with Darling International, Irving, Texas, April 1, 1996.

8. Personal correspondence with Bi-Pro Marketing Limited, Harriston, Ontario, April 2, 1996.

9. "Wheat Is Checked for Toxin after Pet Food Sickens Dogs," Associated Press, August 22, 1995.

10. Phillips, *op. cit.*, pp. 12-17.

11. Anitra Frazier with Norma Eckroate *The New Natural Cat*, New York: Dutton, 1990, p. 52.

12. Wendell O. Belfield and Martin Zucker, *How to Have a Healthier Dog*, New York: Doubleday and Company, 1981, p. 39.

13. Alfred Plechner and Martin Zucker, *Pet Allergies: Remedies for an Epidemic*, Inglewood: Wilshire Book Co., 1986, p. 31.

14. Animal Protection Institute of America, "Investigative Report on Pet Food," *Newsletter*, 1996, p. 5.

15. In Pat Lazarus, *Keep Your Pet Healthy the Natural Way*, New Canaan: Keats Publishing, 1983, p. 6.

16. National Academy of Science, "Nutrient Requirements of Dogs," National Research Council, Washington, D.C., 1974, pp. 17, 18.

17. Personal correspondence with Mann Laboratories, Mississauga, Ontario, July 3, 1990.

18. H. Winter Griffith, *Complete Guide to Vitamins, Minerals and Other Supplements*, Tucson, Arizona: Fisher Books, 1988, p. 49.

19. "Congenital Metabolic Abnormalities," *Dogs In Canada*, August 1992, p. 90.

20. Extoxnet Extension Toxicology Network, "Breakdown of Chemicals in Vegetation," Cornell University, Michigan State University, Oregon State University and University of California at Davis, Paper, May 1994.

21. Animal Protection Institute, *op. cit.*, p. 5.

22. June Wholley, "Ethoxyquin, Facts and Questions," *The German Shepherd Quarterly*, Winter 1990/1991.

23. R.L. Wysong, "Pet Health Alert," Brochure, Wysong Corporation, Midland, Michigan, 1995, pp. 3,4.

24. Ibid.

25. "Odds and Ends," *Wall Street Journal*, April 19, 1993.

26. "Iodine Levels Blamed for Tumors," Petfood Industry, July/August 1996.

27. M.J. Struejer, J.G. Morris, B.F. Feldman, Q.R. Rogers, "Vitamin K. Deficiency in Cats," *The Veterinary Record*, November 16, 1996.

28. "Vexing Feline Problem," *Petfood Industry*, May/June 1996.

29. R.L. Wysong, op. cit., p. 2.

30. Ibid.

31. Animal Protection Institute, *op. cit.*, p. 8.

32. Jim Corbin, "Pet Foods and Feeding," *Feedstuffs*, July 17, 1996, p. 80.

Chapter Five: Hidden Hazards in Pet Foods: Drugs, Heavy Metals, Pesticides, and Pathogens

1. Personal correspondence with Dr. Ashley Robinson, University of Minnesota, August 26, 1994.

2. The Humane Farming Association, 1996, p. 1, citing *Food Chemical News*, DATE TK.

3. Personal correspondence with Don Franco, DVM, with the National Renderers Association, Alexandria, Virginia, March 22, 1995.

4. Personal correspondence with Mark Papich, DVM, MS, North Carolina State University, March 1, 1995.

5. S.F. Sundlof, *Antimicrobial Therapy in Veterinary Medicine*, Ames, Iowa: University of Iowa Press, 1993, p. 575.

6. Ibid., p. 574.

7. Personal correspondence with William Hare, DVM, PhD, National Animal Poison Control Center, Urbana, Illinois, February 13, 1996.

8. L. Maynard and J. Loosli, *Animal Nutrition*, New York: McGraw-Hill, 1969, p. 322.

9. David S. Kronfeld, "Responses to Frequent Questions about Bovine Somatotropin Especially those Provoked by the Posilac Side Effects," Paper, The Office of Technology Assessment, February 15, 1994.

10. Personal correspondence with William Hare, DVM, PhD, National Animal Poison Control Center, Urbana, Illinois, July 30, 1996.

11. *Earthsave Newsletter*, Summer 1996.

12. Wendell O. Belfield and Martin Zucker, *How to Have a Healthier Dog*, New York: Doubleday and Company, 1981, p. 39.

13. Jeff Bender and Ashley Robinson, "Health Concerns Relating to the Feeding of Raw Meat to Companion and Performance Animals," Paper, University of Minnesota: Department of Clinical and Population Sciences, 1994.

14. Farm Sanctuary, "Super Birds and Super Problems," Brochure, Fall 1996.

15. Vicam Microbiological Testing, "Salmonella Screen," Brochure, 1994.

16. "Mycotoxin Costs," *Petfood Industry*, July/August 1996, p. 25.

17. Timothy A. Gbodi, National Veterinary Research Institute, Toxicology Section, Vom, Nigeria, Nwako Nwude, Faculty of Veterinary Medicine, Department of Physiology and Pharmacology, Ahmadu Bello University, Zaria, Nigeria. "Mycotoxicoses in Domestic Animals: A Review," *Vet Hum Toxicol* 30 (3), June 1988.

18. Debora Van Brenk, "Wheat Fungus Epidemic Shows Limited in Science," *London Free Press*, London, Ontario, December 13, 1996.

19. Mann Laboratories, Report, July 3, 1990.

20. Lester Hankin, G.H. Heichel, and Richard Botsford, Paper, "Lead Content of Pet Foods," Connecticut Agricultural Experiment Station, 1975, pp. 630-632.

21. Belfield and Zucker, *op. cit.*, p. 36.

Chapter Six: Pet Food Regulations in the United States and Canada

1. Anonymous, facsimile, January 19, 1997.

2. Personal correspondence with USDA, Animal and Plant Health Inspection Service, Hyattsville Maryland, May 26, 1994.

3. Personal correspondence with the USDA, Food Safety and Inspection Service, Washington, D.C., June 24, 1994.

4. Personal correspondence with the FDA/Center for Veterinary Medicine, March 7, 1995.

5. Personal correspondence with Stephen F. Sundlof, DVM, PhD. Director, Center for Veterinary Medicine, March 7, 1995.

6. "Understanding Pet Food Labels," *FDA Consumer*, Vol. 28, No. 8, October 1994, p. 12.

7. Personal correspondence with Carol Barfield, United Animal Owners Association, Cleveland, Ohio, January 9, 1995.

8. "Ethoxyquin Study Results," *Petfood Industry*, May/June 1996.

9. *FDA Consumer*, op. cit., p. 12.

10. Association of American Feed Control Officials, Ingredient Definitions, 1994.

11. Department of Natural Resources, State of Alaska, January 12, 1995; Florida Department of Agriculture and Consumer Services, January 5, 1995.

12. Personal correspondence with Don Franco, DVM, National Renderers Association, August 14, 1995.

13. Personal correspondence with Darling International, April 1, 1996.

14. Brochures, Pet Food Rules and Regulations: Massachusetts Department of Agriculture; Mississippi Commercial Feed Law of 1972; Missouri Commercial Feed Law; New Mexico Commercial Feed Law; Senate Bill No. 729, Session of 1993, The General Assembly of Pennsylvania; Rhode Island Commercial Feed Law; Vermont Feed Regulations.

15. Jill Carey, "Negotiating the Cat Food Jungle," *Cats*, November 1996, p. 38.

16. "Putting the Pieces Together," *The Pet Dealer*, July 1992, p. 48.

17. Personal correspondence with the Department of Agriculture, State of Missouri, January 6, 1995.

18. Personal correspondence with the Honorable Tom Hockin, PC, MP, Ottawa, Ontario, October 10, 1990.

19. Personal correspondence with the Honorable Elmer Buchanan, MPP, February 27, 1991.

20. Personal correspondence with the Honorable Charles Meyer, Minister of Agriculture, Ottawa, Ontario, February 8, 1993.

21. Personal correspondence with Dr. I. Kirk, Agriculture Canada, Ottawa, Ontario, September 9, 1993.

22. Personal correspondence with the Honorable Ralph Goodale, Minister of Agriculture, Ottawa, Ontario, May 30, 1994.

23. Ibid.

24. Personal correspondence with the Honorable John Manley, Minister of Industry, Ottawa, Ontario, July 11, 1994.

25. The Canadian Veterinary Medical Association, Pet Food Certification Program, 1989.

26. Personal correspondence with the Canadian Veterinary Medical Association, Ottawa, Ontario, August 5, 1994.

27. Pet Food Association of Canada, "Nutrition Assurance Program," Brochure, Mississauga, Ontario, 1990.

28. Personal correspondence with the Ministry of Food and Agriculture, Toronto, Ontario, March 15, 1995; personal correspondence with Agriculture and Agri-Food Canada, Nepean, Ontario, March 30, 1995.

29. Personal correspondence with the Pet Food Association of Canada, Mississauga, Ontario, March 28, 1995.

30. Pet Food Association to *The Toronto Star*, Document, January 18, 1993.

Chapter Seven: Recipes and Other Helpful Hints for a Healthy Pet

1. Wendell Belfield and Martin Zucker, *How to Have a Healthier Dog*, New York: Doubleday and Company, 1981, p. 42.

2. Catherine O'Driscoll and John Watt, *Canine Health Census*, Langor, Derbyshire England, 1996.

3. Pat Lazarus, *Keep Your Pet Healthy the Natural Way*, New Canaan, Connecticut: Keats Publishing, 1993, pp. 21-37.

4. Ibid., pp. 30, 31.

5. Ibid., p. 31.

6. Belfield and Zucker, op. cit., pp. 51, 52.

7. Ibid., p. 159.

8. Ibid.

9. Catherine O'Driscoll, "A Can of Worms at the Flea Circus," *Canine Health Census*, Longnor, Derbyshire, 1996.

10. Belfield and Zucker, *op. cit.*, p. 212.

11. Howard M. Hayes, Robert E. Tarone, Kenneth P. Cantor, Carl R. Jessen, Dennis M. McCurnin, Ralph C. Richardson, "2,4-Dichlorphenoxyacetic Acid," *Journal of the National Cancer Institute*, Vol. 83, No. 17, September 4, 1991.

12. Rachel's Hazardous Waste News #5, "Cancer Causing Weed Killer May Endanger Farmers, Suburbanites," Paper, Annapolis, Maryland: Environmental Research Foundation, December 29, 1986.

Chapter Eight: Resources for Consumer Action

1. "Lifetime Value of Pets," *Petfood Industry*, March/April 1996, pp. 20, 21.

2. Animal Protection Institute of America, "Investigative Report on Pet Food," *Newsletter*, 1996, p. 11.

3. Michele Jachim, "Coordinating Resources," *Petfood Industry*, May/June 1996, p. 4 .

4. Pet Food Association of Canada, Brochure, Mississauga, Ontario.

5. Animal Protection Institute of America, *op. cit.*, p. 13.

6. "The AAFCO Challenge," *Petfood Industry*, January/February 1997, pp. 38, 39.

7. Ibid.

8. Tim Phillips, "Scandal Hungry?" *Petfood Industry*, November/December 1996, p. 47.

9. Ibid.

10. Ibid.

11. Ibid

12. Ibid.

13. Personal correspondence with April Cummings, "eye.tv," Austin, Texas, November 18, 1996.

14. Petfood Forum 96, Advertisement in *Petfood Industry*, March/April 1996, pp. 20, 21.

INDEX

Books by NewSage Press

Eating with Conscience: The Bioethics of Food
Dr. Michael W. Fox

The Wolf, the Woman, the Wilderness: A True Story of
  Returning Home
Teresa tsimmu Martino

Dancer on the Grass: True Stories of Horses and People
Teresa tsimmu Martino
(Available Summer 1998)

Animals as Teachers & Healers: True Stories & Reflections
Susan Chernak McElroy
(first published by NewSage, now available through Ballantine)

One Woman, One Vote: Rediscovering the Woman
  Suffrage Movement
edited by Marjorie Spruill Wheeler

Jailed for Freedom: American Women Win the Vote
Doris Stevens, edited by Carol O'Hare

Women & Work: In Their Own Words
edited by Maureen R. Michelson

Blue Moon Over Thurman Street
Ursula K. Le Guin
Photographs by Roger Dorband

When the Bough Breaks: Pregnancy & the Legacy of Addiction
Kira Corser & Frances Payne Adler

A Portrait of American Mothers & Daughters
Raisa Fastman

Organizing for Our Lives: New Voices from Rural Communities
Richard Steven Street & Samuel Orozco

Family Portraits in Changing Times
Helen Nestor

Stories of Adoption: Loss & Reunion
Eric Blau, M.D.

Common Heroes: Facing a Life Threatening Illness
Eric Blau, M.D.